Memories Volume 1

Vernon Coleman

Vernon Coleman: What the papers say

'Vernon Coleman writes brilliant books.' – The Good Book Guide
'No thinking person can ignore him.' – The Ecologist
'The calmest voice of reason.' – The Observer
'A godsend.' – Daily Telegraph
'Superstar.' – Independent on Sunday
'Brilliant!' – The People
'Compulsive reading.' – The Guardian
'His message is important.' – The Economist
'He's the Lone Ranger, Robin Hood and the Equalizer rolled into one.' – Glasgow Evening Times
'The man is a national treasure.' – What Doctors Don't Tell You
'His advice is optimistic and enthusiastic.' – British Medical Journal
'Revered guru of medicine.' – Nursing Times
'Gentle, kind and caring' – Western Daily Press
'His trademark is that he doesn't mince words. Far funnier than the usual tone of soupy piety you get from his colleagues.' – The Guardian
'Dr Coleman is one of our most enlightened, trenchant and sensitive dispensers of medical advice.' – The Observer
'I would much rather spend an evening in his company than be trapped for five minutes in a radio commentary box with Mr Geoffrey Boycott.' – Peter Tinniswood, Punch
'Hard hitting...inimitably forthright.' – Hull Daily Mail
'Refreshingly forthright.' – Liverpool Daily Post
'Outspoken and alert.' – Sunday Express
'Dr Coleman made me think again.' – BBC World Service
'Marvellously succinct, refreshingly sensible.' – The Spectator
'Probably one of the most brilliant men alive today.' – Irish Times
'King of the media docs.' – The Independent
'Britain's leading medical author.' – The Star
'Britain's leading health care campaigner.' – The Sun
'Perhaps the best known health writer for the general public in the world today.' – The Therapist
'The patient's champion.' – Birmingham Post

'A persuasive writer whose arguments, based on research and experience, are sound.' – Nursing Standard
'The doctor who dares to speak his mind.' – Oxford Mail
'He writes lucidly and wittily.' – Good Housekeeping

Books by Vernon Coleman include:

Medical
The Medicine Men
Paper Doctors
Everything You Want To Know About Ageing
The Home Pharmacy
Aspirin or Ambulance
Face Values
Stress and Your Stomach
A Guide to Child Health
Guilt
The Good Medicine Guide
An A to Z of Women's Problems
Bodypower
Bodysense
Taking Care of Your Skin
Life without Tranquillisers
High Blood Pressure
Diabetes
Arthritis
Eczema and Dermatitis
The Story of Medicine
Natural Pain Control
Mindpower
Addicts and Addictions
Dr Vernon Coleman's Guide to Alternative Medicine
Stress Management Techniques
Overcoming Stress
The Health Scandal
The 20 Minute Health Check
Sex for Everyone
Mind over Body
Eat Green Lose Weight
Why Doctors Do More Harm Than Good
The Drugs Myth

Complete Guide to Sex
How to Conquer Backache
How to Conquer Pain
Betrayal of Trust
Know Your Drugs
Food for Thought
The Traditional Home Doctor
Relief from IBS
The Parent's Handbook
Men in Bras, Panties and Dresses
Power over Cancer
How to Conquer Arthritis
How to Stop Your Doctor Killing You
Superbody
Stomach Problems – Relief at Last
How to Overcome Guilt
How to Live Longer
Coleman's Laws
Millions of Alzheimer Patients Have Been Misdiagnosed
Climbing Trees at 112
Is Your Health Written in the Stars?
The Kick-Ass A–Z for over 60s
Briefs Encounter
The Benzos Story
Dementia Myth
Waiting

Psychology/Sociology
Stress Control
How to Overcome Toxic Stress
Know Yourself (1988)
Stress and Relaxation
People Watching
Spiritpower
Toxic Stress
I Hope Your Penis Shrivels Up
Oral Sex: Bad Taste and Hard To Swallow
Other People's Problems

The 100 Sexiest, Craziest, Most Outrageous Agony Column Questions (and Answers) Of All Time
How to Relax and Overcome Stress
Too Sexy To Print
Psychiatry
Are You Living With a Psychopath?

Politics and General
England Our England
Rogue Nation
Confronting the Global Bully
Saving England
Why Everything Is Going To Get Worse Before It Gets Better
The Truth They Won't Tell You...About The EU
Living In a Fascist Country
How to Protect & Preserve Your Freedom, Identity & Privacy
Oil Apocalypse
Gordon is a Moron
The OFPIS File
What Happens Next?
Bloodless Revolution
2020
Stuffed
The Shocking History of the EU
Coming Apocalypse
Covid-19: The Greatest Hoax in History
Old Man in a Chair
Endgame
Proof that Masks do more Harm than Good
Covid-19: The Fraud Continues
Covid-19: Exposing the Lies

Diaries
Diary of a Disgruntled Man
Just another Bloody Year
Bugger off and Leave Me Alone
Return of the Disgruntled Man
Life on the Edge
The Game's Afoot

Tickety Tonk

Animals
Why Animal Experiments Must Stop
Fighting For Animals
Alice and Other Friends
Animal Rights – Human Wrongs
Animal Experiments – Simple Truths

General Non Fiction
How to Publish Your Own Book
How to Make Money While Watching TV
Strange but True
Daily Inspirations
Why Is Public Hair Curly
People Push Bottles Up Peaceniks
Secrets of Paris
Moneypower
101 Things I Have Learned
100 Greatest Englishmen and Englishwomen
Cheese Rolling, Shin Kicking and Ugly Tattoos
One Thing after Another

Novels (General)
Mrs Caldicot's Cabbage War
Mrs Caldicot's Knickerbocker Glory
Mrs Caldicot's Oyster Parade
Mrs Caldicot's Turkish Delight
Deadline
Second Chance
Tunnel
Mr Henry Mulligan
The Truth Kills
Revolt
My Secret Years with Elvis
Balancing the Books
Doctor in Paris
Stories with a Twist in the Tale (short stories)
Dr Bullock's Annals

The Young Country Doctor Series
Bilbury Chronicles
Bilbury Grange
Bilbury Revels
Bilbury Country
Bilbury Village
Bilbury Pie (short stories)
Bilbury Pudding (short stories)
Bilbury Tonic
Bilbury Relish
Bilbury Mixture
Bilbury Delights
Bilbury Joys
Bilbury Tales
Bilbury Days
Bilbury Memories

Novels (Sport)
Thomas Winsden's Cricketing Almanack
Diary of a Cricket Lover
The Village Cricket Tour
The Man Who Inherited a Golf Course
Around the Wicket
Too Many Clubs and Not Enough Balls

Cat books
Alice's Diary
Alice's Adventures
We Love Cats
Cats Own Annual
The Secret Lives of Cats
Cat Basket
The Cataholics' Handbook
Cat Fables
Cat Tales
Catoons from Catland

As Edward Vernon

Practice Makes Perfect
Practise What You Preach
Getting Into Practice
Aphrodisiacs – An Owner's Manual
The Complete Guide to Life

Written with Donna Antoinette Coleman
How to Conquer Health Problems between Ages 50 & 120
Health Secrets Doctors Share With Their Families
Animal Miscellany
England's Glory
Wisdom of Animals

Copyright Vernon Coleman February 2022
The right of Vernon Coleman to be identified as the author of this work has been asserted in accordance with the Copyright, Designs and Patents Act 1988.

Dedication

To My Wife, Sweetheart and Friend Antoinette, as ever.
I love you with my heart, mind and spirit. You are with me everywhere and eternally the greater part of me. Always and all ways.

Contents List

Introduction
Why I Resigned
Private Doctor
Walking Around in Circles
An Old Lady
Robert Donat: What do I Require from Life?
Mrs Caldicot: The Premiere
How a Cat Called Alice Changed My life
George and Millie
The Scary Phone Box
Helping Out a Friend
Another Scary Story
A Kindness
CB Fry
An English Gentleman
Columns Galore
An Editor
At the Ritz
The Magician
Mickey Spillane
Literary Agents
Circus Clowns
Cars
The Big Sleep
Police Surgeon
Duncan
Childhood
Kirkby
An Odd Couple
Television Days
Home Visit
McBain
Jimmy
Journalism
The Policeman's Wife

Vadim
Mountaineer
The Hat Dance
Napoleon
Trivia in Medicine
Idiomatic English in France
Fear
Touring
Walnuts
My Life as Edward Vernon
My Career in the Movies
Anton
The Policeman's Shoulder
Old Age
Parties
Time
A Night at the Cavern
The First Television
My Networking Skills
Keith Miller
The Gallows

Extra 1: The Best Diaries
Extra 2: Books to Read
Extra 3: Biography of the Author
Extra 4: References
Extra 5: A Note about the Typeface

Introduction

I've always been suspicious of autobiographies which start with neat memories of schooldays, progress through early adulthood and end up at some later point with every achievement and experience neatly recorded. And I am always impressed by people who keep diaries which enable them to see where they were on April 2nd 1962, who they dined with and how much they tipped the waiter. I'm afraid that from where I am sitting life doesn't seem like that.

Looking back is, for me, like rummaging through the attic, finding bits and pieces and going 'Oh, gosh, fancy that!' a great deal. I'm constantly alternating happy thoughts with memories of disappointments.

Most of my memories aren't neatly defined, with a reason, an ambition and a denouement. Most of my memories flash back in no particular order and are apparent more as bitty stories and anecdotes. Sometimes a memory from ten years ago pops up. And sometimes I remember something from fifty years ago. As a result, the true stories and anecdotes in this book are in absolutely no logical order; instead they are in the order in which they tumbled out of my head. I could have forced them into some sort of order, or characterised them according to theme, but that would have been entirely artificial. I could have tied all the bits together and called it a traditional autobiography but it would seem to me like tipping a dish of hors d'oeuvres into a dish and calling it a stew. Or pouring a plateful of petits fours into a dish and calling the result a trifle. Why would you? In my experience, life doesn't necessarily move forward in a nice, neat straight line. Old memories don't always stay where you put them.

Apart from a seven year period during my late 60s and early 70s, I have no diaries to look back on. And those seven diaries have already been published in their entirety. (Just in case you are interested the titles are *Diary of a Disgruntled Man, Just Another Bloody Year, Bugger Off And Leave Me Alone, The Return of the Disgruntled Man, Life on the Edge, The Game's Afoot* and *Tickety Tonk*.)

But I'm not really bothered by the absence of any old diaries because I have always found that biographies which are built upon a strict structure of dates, times and places tend to be rather dull and disappointing.

Similarly, I have also found autobiographies which are built around celebrities (and their carefully rehearsed clever sayings) are dull, disappointing and invariably rather self-serving. No one is going to be interested, for example, in the fact that Dudley Moore and I once slept together. (We were sitting together on the TV AM sofa. Warm lights and an advertising break resulted in us both nodding off, and that provides all the explanation anyone needs. But it's a good example of how misleading headlines can be created.)

However, although I may not be able to remember bare facts I can remember how I felt, what I thought, what I learnt and what I did wrong at the important times of my life.

And so this is a book of personal impressions, confessions, experiences, anecdotes and feelings. The mixture is spiced with a few regrets too.

I have worked in the media and in medicine for over half a century (sometimes separately, sometimes not) and I have met a good many people. I am not, however, going to invade anyone's privacy or cause hurt or embarrassment to people I have known or even met only briefly. I am much more enthusiastic about re-telling true stories and anecdotes which seem to be odd, amusing or revealing. Where it is necessary to protect the privacy of someone (whether alive or dead) I have changed names.

Some people are in our lives permanently, some are present for a while (often intensely) and then disappear for one reason or another, a few come and go into and out of our lives like the seasons (but not so regularly) and others wander into and then out of our lives in what seems, in retrospect, to be an instant but nevertheless leaves an indelible, eternal mark for some reason.

And so I have defied convention by writing this book in apparently disconnected chapters. It is, I hope, one of those books which can be read at a single sitting, used as a bedside book or dipped into and out of like one of those commonplace books the Victorians liked so much.

This is a look back on long years of happiness, frustration and disappointment, mildly raised hopes rather than vivid ambitions, a feeling of always being outside, nose pressed against the glass, watching the smooth, the confident, the comfortable and the belonging and wondering why it is that I have always felt myself to be an outsider. I've always felt that the smooth and the belonging have always regarded me as an outsider and sneered at whatever I did. I doubt if that is a unique feeling.

We all like to think we can carve a slice of immortality for ourselves. Parents hope to do it through their children, politicians through their rhetoric and self-serving autobiographies, architects through the buildings they design, soldiers through the battles they win, artists through the work they've exhibited, authors through their books, actors through their performances and sportsmen through great victories or records.

But most of us are kidding ourselves, of course.

Children eventually die and then their children die. Most achievements melt into history's melting pot. Companies and institutions, once grand and much admired, are taken over or broken up or simply fade away. Buildings fall down or are knocked down. For every Pyramid or Stonehenge there are a million less memorable edifices. And of those which stand for centuries how many people know the names of the architects? Battles are mostly forgotten unless they are failures (the charge of the Light Brigade) or romantic (Trafalgar). Only half a dozen painters, composers or authors per century will be remembered: chosen at random names such as Shakespeare, Dickens, Twain, Goethe, Dumas, Proust, Turner, Rembrandt, Renoir, Mozart and Beethoven spring into the mind but how many others are now forgotten – except perhaps for academics looking for minor influences to fill out a thesis? The vast majority of actors fade as their films go out of date. Sporting exploits are forgotten except by dedicated followers of a particular sport. Time is the great destroyer. So we should live in the now and be satisfied with that.

So, to sum up, the pieces in this book are miscellaneous memories, flashes of thought, snatches of anecdotes, and experiences which seemed worth rescuing and restoring to some sort of life. Nearly everything in here took place back in the 20th century and early 21st century. None of it took place during the lunacies which characterised the years from 2020 onwards. And parts of the book are (and are intended to be) the sort of things likely to have appeared in a Victorian Gentleman's Commonplace book.

Remember, my memories are included in the order in which they occurred to me. I haven't checked dates or names because as someone (I think it was Anthony Burgess) once said: 'Reality is what I remember.' Or, at least, that's what I seem to remember him saying when critics accused him of making up much of the material included in his autobiography. So, please do not expect any logic in the way in which these pieces appear.

Preston Sturges, the great American film director, once planned a book entitled 'Various Events Leading Up to this Point in my Life'. That sums up this book perfectly.

Many of my books are intended primarily to educate, though with the hope that the reader will also be entertained. This book is primarily intended to entertain and if the reader finds nuggets of information or advice then that's a bonus.

If this book proves successful (and to a writer that simply means 'if enough people want to read it') then this is the first in a series of reminiscences. If the book isn't successful (in writer's terms) then this is my first and last book of miscellaneous reminiscences.

The one certain thing I have learned about writing books is that you just never know.

Vernon Coleman
Bilbury, January 2022

Note

Censors can rest easy for (by choice) there is nothing in this book about the events which dominated the world from 2020 onwards. Most of the events in this book took place long ago, and they are none the worse for that.

Why I Resigned

Among the multitude of lies about me on the internet (many of them so bizarre they deserve to be classified as science fiction – 'I read it on the internet' is slightly less reliable than 'I heard it from the women who does the teas at the football club, and she got it from her brother-in-law who heard it from the man who delivers free papers') there is one claiming that I left medical practice after my first book *The Medicine Men* was published. The book was about the relationship between the medical profession and the drug industry and although it does make regular appearances in bibliographies at the back of other people's books, it has been out of print for decades.

The Medicine Men was published in 1975 and I received an advance of £750 to write it. The typist who worked on the typescript charged £800 and the insurers from whom I bought libel insurance charged me £700.

I received a little money for foreign rights (I think the Italian edition may still be in print), book club rights and mass market paperback rights but the book wasn't ever going to allow me to take off to the Bahamas to live on a huge yacht. Financially, I think I just about broke even on the book.

I didn't resign as a GP until seven or eight years later.

Being a GP was the job I'd always wanted to do and one that I enjoyed a great deal. I enjoyed seeing patients. But I wasn't terribly keen on all the administration – which was, of course, nowhere near as bad then as it is now, but which was annoying and time consuming.

In those distant days, GPs in England were responsible for their patients 365 days a year and 24 hours a day. So that we had some time off, most doctors worked in informal groups of four or five. Often the association was a very loose one in that individual GPs ran their practices independently and merely shared their out of hours' responsibilities. It all worked surprisingly well and easily.

If there were five doctors sharing their night time, weekend and bank holiday calls then each one of the five would be on call one night a week and one weekend in five. It wasn't particularly onerous though these days young doctors would look at you as if you were mad if you suggested that they take on such extra responsibilities.

But the system we had then worked far better than the chaotic system which has replaced it – and which has left patients having to choose between calling an ambulance, and preparing themselves for a lengthy wait in a casualty department (a wait which can easily stretch to twelve hours) or telephoning a not terribly impressive Government run help-line for advice. If you have the money, of course, you can always contact a doctor via the internet. The irony is that the doctor you speak to will be someone else's GP, doing a few out of hours extra work for a fat fee. None of these individuals (the casualty doctor, the person answering the telephone call or the moonlighting GP) will know anything about you, your health problems or your family history.

Politicians and today's doctors will doubtless disagree with me but I firmly believe the old system was much better.

I never particularly minded out of hours calls. Indeed, the best bit of being a GP was driving back home at 4.00 am having spent an hour or two successfully treating a patient at home. It might have been an asthmatic having severe trouble breathing and needing intravenous injections or a child screaming with pain from an ear infection. It was proper medicine, just a doctor and a patient: no need for a referral, no investigations, no paperwork.

Of course, the glow of satisfaction might dim slightly if, when getting back home, I found there was another call to be done. If there were another call then it would inevitably be to a house in the next street to the one I'd just left. There were no mobile phones those days; they were a mixed blessing yet to be invented.

After a night on call we still did morning surgery, of course. And that was sometimes a little tiring. I wasn't the only GP to fall asleep in his consulting room.

So why, after just ten years, did I give up my dream job?

It was the paperwork, the bureaucracy, which defeated me.

One of a GP's tasks was to sign sick notes. And the law required doctors to put the diagnosis on the form. The patient then took the form to their employer. Inevitably, this meant that everyone in the office knew what the patient's problem was.

One of my patients was the manager of the local branch of a big chain store.

He came in to see me one day and it wasn't difficult to diagnose the problem. He was severely depressed; worn down by demanding bosses and a difficult job. He needed time off work.

I reached for the sick note pad, scribbled his name and address and then wrote 'depression' in the box requiring a diagnosis.

'Do you have to put that down?' he asked.

I looked at him, puzzled.

'If my bosses see that then I'll be fired,' he told me.

I ripped up the form and wrote another. On this one I scribbled 'virus infection'.

A couple of days later, a young woman came to see me. She was pregnant and was suffering from morning sickness.

'Do you mind not putting down that I'm pregnant?' she asked. 'The girls at work don't know but I have to hand the form in to my boss.'

And so she had a virus infection too.

After that all the sick notes I signed contained the same diagnosis: virus infection.

After a few weeks of this I was hauled before a local National Health Service committee – one given the responsibility of regulating family doctors. They had a sheaf of sick notes I had signed. All the forms had the same diagnosis. My, were they cross. None of the committee members had any sympathy or understanding. I'd broken the rules and there was unforgiveness in the air.

To cut a long story short they fined me a couple of hundred pounds and threatened to do it again and again if I didn't write down proper diagnoses. £200 was a lot of money in those days (it's a lot of money now but it was more then).

So I resigned from my job as a GP and became a professional writer.

Shortly afterwards, I'm pleased to say, the rules were changed and patients were allowed to write their own sick notes.

Private Doctor

After I resigned from my job as a GP in the National Health Service (a job most doctors regard as being a 'job for life') I thought I ought to find a part-time job in medicine so that I could keep my hand in, so to speak. Even though I was going to spend most of my time writing I didn't want to lose touch with practical medicine completely.

And so, a week or so after I retired, I replied to an advert I had seen in a medical magazine. A doctor in private practice was looking for an assistant to work one day a week. He wanted someone to do a surgery in the morning and another in the evening. The only snag was that the surgery was 20 miles away from where I was living at the time. Since it wasn't worth driving all the way home, and all the way back, I simply drove into the centre of the town, sat in a local café, had some lunch and did some work on whatever book I was writing at the time.

There were a couple of unusual things about the practice.

The first was that the doctor kept a well-stocked pharmacy and dispensed all the drugs he prescribed. These days quite a number of doctors run their own dispensing pharmacy as a lucrative side-line but in those days the only GPs who dispensed their own prescriptions tended to live and work in remote country areas – usually miles from the nearest town and the nearest chemists shop. But since the GP I was working for was in private practice, and outside the restrictions of the health service, he could pretty well choose to do whatever he wanted to do.

The second oddity was that everything was paid for in cash. I can't remember what the exact fees were but I wouldn't be far out if I guessed that the fee for a consultation was a standard £20 and that there was an additional fee for any medicine that was prescribed. There was a price list pinned up in the dispensary so that I knew what to charge for medicines.

I'm writing about 1984 and that £20 would be worth around £50 today – that's a fairly low price for a face to face consultation with a private doctor, though you might get an internet consultation slightly cheaper, I suppose.

There was another oddity. Instead of paying me a fixed fee for each surgery (the usual way of doing things) the doctor I was working for suggested that we simply split the consultation fees between us. He received £10 per patient because it was his practice and he provided the rooms, the receptionist, the telephone and the heat and light and I got to keep the other £10 for seeing the patient. He obviously received the money paid for any drugs prescribed.

The financial advantage of this system was that the more patients I saw, the more money I earned. The financial disadvantage was that if no patients turned up, I sat there for two hours and went home empty handed.

In practice, I don't think I ever had a surgery that didn't have ten patients in it and there were sometimes as many as 15. Each consultation lasted as long as was required and patients, who just turned up at the advertised times, simply sat in the waiting room until their name was called.

There were several reasons why the practice succeeded.

First, the local NHS practices had long waiting lists for appointments. If you wanted to see a doctor you had to wait two to three weeks. If you had an urgent problem you might get seen within a week. There was no waiting time at the practice where I was working.

Second, we didn't have an appointments system. If you wanted to see a doctor you came into the surgery, you gave your name to the receptionist, you sat down and you waited. If you'd been seen before there would be a medical records envelope with details of your medical history. Whatever the administrators may think, most patients prefer this sort of system.

Third, you weren't rushed in and out of the surgery in the standard two minutes allowed by many NHS practices.

Fourth (and I am a bit nervous about mentioning it but it's true, so I will) none of the local NHS GPs spoke English terribly well. They spoke some English, of course. But they didn't speak it very well. For most of them English was their second language. And patients preferred to see a doctor they could converse with easily, without having to think of three ways to say the same thing. I'm nervous about mentioning this because there are some who will say that the patients were being racist. Or that I am being racist in mentioning it. But they weren't and I'm not. I don't think any of them gave a damn where the doctor was born or trained. They just wanted to be able to share their intimate secrets as quickly and as easily as they could in the language they knew best. For the record, the doctor I was working for was of Asian origin. He had, however, been trained in the UK and he spoke impeccable English.

At the end of a busy surgery I would have a few hundred pounds stuffed in the desk drawer. I'd deduct the money paid for medicines, leave half for the absent principal and take my share home with me. The receptionist kept a track of the money because she had a list of the number of patients I'd seen – and every patient paid the same amount. The owner of the practice didn't have to worry about his employee cheating him.

Doing two surgeries a day meant that my earnings were between £0 (meaning that I was out the cost of petrol, lunch and my time) and £300 or so. The top end may sound a lot but it was far less than I was earning writing books, columns and articles and appearing on TV programmes. And I'd have earned more from medicine if I'd stayed on as a GP and put up with the bureaucracy.

'What do you do with all the cash?' I asked the proprietor of the practice. 'How often do you take it to the bank? Do you ever have in trouble paying in loads of notes?'

He looked at me a little furtively. 'I bank half of it,' he confessed.

'What do you do with the other half?' I asked, innocently.

'I go to London once every couple of months.'

'Oh,' I said, assuming he meant that he went to London and had a really good time.

'And buy stamps,' he added.

'Stamps?' I repeated, wondering why the devil he went all the way to London to buy stamps when there was a perfectly adequate Post Office just two hundreds away from the surgery.

'Rare stamps,' he whispered. 'From a dealer in The Strand.'

'You buy the stamps with the cash?' I said, catching on at last.

He nodded.

'I used to buy jewellery,' he said. 'I've got a good collection of watches. Patek Philippe, old Rolex, stuff like that. There are dealers who specialise in selling second hand watches. But I decided that the mark-up on jewellery is too high. I might as well pay the tax.'

I admired his courage but I took my cash to the bank, paid it all into my account and declared it.

I did wonder why he confessed this crime to me.

And then, a few days later, I realised he hadn't been confessing. He'd been boasting.

In the end I left because a patient rang up and demanded that I leave a prescription for a colleague to pick up for him. I didn't know the patient at all. And I said I'd need to see him first. He got angry and threatened to complain to my employer. I said that was fine but that I wouldn't give him a prescription unless I saw him. Minutes later the boss rang me and shouted at me for not doing as the caller had demanded.

I told him that I would finish the surgery but that I wouldn't be returning. We didn't have a contract so it was easy. After the last patient had been seen I took my income for the day and went home.

The doctor rang me at home the next day and asked me to change my mind. But I didn't. My days as a private doctor were over. They'd lasted less than six months.

I never picked up a stethoscope in anger after that.

I had seen my last, real-life patient.

My one medical regret was that I never found a little single-handed practice somewhere in the middle of nowhere or on a tiny island, perhaps one of those windswept ones off the coast of Scotland.

That would have been my dream-job.

A single-handed medical practice in a remote, rural region. No partners, no need for staff. Just a house big enough to provide a room I could use as a consulting room and a room to use as a waiting room.

I still sometimes wonder what it would have been like.

And deep down I don't think I've entirely given up on the idea.

Walking Around in Circles

When I became a GP I took over a single handed practice in a small town, which had been run for over 40 years by a rather truculent but good-hearted Scotsman. I call it a single-handed practice because technically it was but he had a working relationship with two other practices in the town. This meant that the members of the three practices could share their evening and weekend rota duties.

My predecessor had run his practice from two downstairs rooms in the terraced house where he lived. He carried on living in the upstairs portion of the house and I took over the consulting room (which had, many years before, been the dining-room) and the waiting room (which would have been the sitting-room if the house had been arranged more normally).

Together with the receptionist/secretary, whom I had inherited with the practice, I spent much of my first week sorting through the drawers and cupboards and burning or dumping a huge amount of stuff that my predecessor didn't want, and had left behind, and that I certainly had no use for. The receptionist/secretary seemed to me to be about 150-years-old, though she was probably a little younger than this, and she had been with the practice since the dawn of time.

She was slightly scatty and panicked easily but she was invaluable since she was the only person in the world who understood how the filing system for the patients' records was designed and constructed and how it worked. In her absence it was quite impossible to find any medical records at all and anyone who assumed that the filing was done alphabetically by name or address was doomed to failure. Alan Turing would not have worked it out.

In those days medical records were kept on bits of cardboard in a cardboard envelope. They were written in ink. Patients who visited the surgery often, or who had chronic illnesses often had bulging records which were an inch or more thick. Occasionally, I would go through the notes and throw out for burning all the unnecessary duplicates of referral letters and letters from hospital consultants.

I once had trouble with an NHS inspector who arrived and

demanded to take away all the records to be analysed for some reason or other. Since this would have meant trying to run the practice without any records I told him he couldn't take the records away. He pointed to a line at the bottom of each card which said 'Property of the NHS'. Remembering Shakespeare's Merchant of Venice I appeared to relent and told him that he could take the record cards but that he would have to leave the ink behind because the ink was mine. He was very puzzled by this but after some harrumphing and a few threats he disappeared and never came back. I always had a consistent hate/hate relationship with all medical administrators.

When I took over the practice, my panicky secretary and I sorted through cupboards full of old prescription pads, out-of-date sick notes, books full of death certificate stubs and nothing else, notepads provided by drug company representatives which carried advertisements for antibiotics, anti-depressants and a number of different proprietary tonics and cheap ballpoint pens emblazoned with advertisements for products that had long since been superseded or withdrawn from sale. There were dozens and dozens of gifts and gadgets. Golf balls which carried the name of a drug company and the name of one of their products, sheets of blotting paper, calendars going back to just after the Second World War, diaries that might be useful if 1953 ever comes back, bottles which had once contained ink but which now contained a blue-black sludge, invitations to dinners and luncheons, old newspapers and magazines given away by publishers who made their money out of selling advertising to drug companies, half a decade's worth of rolled up copies of the *British Medical Journal* which had never been opened, a boxful of little plastic gadgets for which I could not perceive no use nor value, pen torches with their batteries rotting and measuring tapes. In a drawer I found two old stethoscopes which had tubing that had rotted and an ophthalmoscope that looked as if it had been dropped and would never work again.

I found an old oil drum, and the receptionist and I began a bonfire that lasted for three days. I filled my predecessor's two metal dustbins, rusty but serviceable, with the stuff which didn't look as if it would burn.

My predecessor had never used an appointments system and I didn't either. Things were very simple in those days. Patients turned up at the advertised surgery times and they waited to be seen. Everyone was seen within an hour or two of arriving. Patients were given a number so that they knew where they were in the queue. Many would take a number (provided I seem to remember with the aid of a roll of raffle tickets) and then, having judged how long they would have to wait, would totter to the local shops. The system worked incredibly well and was very simple. There was no need for patients to ring up, we didn't need a huge appointments book, there was no problem with emergencies or requests for an urgent appointment and everyone was seen when they needed to be seen. There were no three week waits for an appointment.

This worked too well of course and so eventually, strict orders came down from on high that I had to introduce an appointment system. The patients, who now had to ring up and fix an appointment hated it and so did I not least because I had to put in another phone line and hire two more receptionists to answer the calls and deal with all the paperwork, but the bureaucrats, who hate all patients and loathe doctors, were very happy with the appointment system and thought it as much fun as a bowl of sticky toffee pudding with a big dollop of whipped cream on top.

I quickly discovered that my now retired predecessor had a couple of quirks.

First, he had prescribed high blood pressure tablets for almost all the 2,500 patients in the practice. I have no idea why he did this. A normal blood pressure is usually regarded as being 120 over 80, with the figure of 120 being the systolic pressure and the figure of 80 being the diastolic pressure. At the time it was usually thought that patients only needed tablets if their diastolic pressure was over 100. However, I think there might have been a little confusion somewhere along the line because my predecessor had given tablets to everyone with a systolic pressure over 100. Since most of these people had perfectly normal blood pressure, which the drugs had lowered to an uncomfortable degree, the result was that I was constantly besieged by patients complaining that they were dizzy and kept falling over. Things weren't helped by the fact that the sphygmomanometer which I had inherited was woefully inaccurate. Indeed, it was so inaccurate that it was entirely useless and I put it into one of the bins together with the plastic gadgets, perished stethoscopes and bags of slightly used urine sample bottles which had, for some reason, been stored in one of the cupboards and which were, I discovered, the source of a noticeable aroma.

I obtained a new blood pressure machine and managed to cure my patients' hypotension by taking them off their entirely unnecessary tablets. This did my reputation no harm at all. I did not want to suggest that my predecessor was in some way incompetent, or flaky, and so I told everyone that their course of treatment had proved successful, that they were cured and that they could therefore stop taking the tablets. They were all very grateful.

Second, for some reason which I never got close to understanding, my now retired predecessor had also told most of his patients (who had now become my patients) to have their shoes fitted with a raise on one side. This was sometimes done with an addition to the heel of a shoe and sometimes done with something called an inner raise – a piece of soft rubber or some other squishy material which was placed inside the shoe and which must have been terribly uncomfortable. The choice of shoe to be raised seemed to be arbitrary with some having their right shoe dealt with and some having the left shoe adapted. Naturally, those who had more than one pair of shoes were put to some considerable expense because all these adaptations fell outside the remit of the National Health Service. The result of these changes was all the patients walked round in circles. Try walking with one shoe higher than the other and you'll see what I mean. Since the patients with the raised shoes were also receiving high blood pressure tablets which they didn't need, the result was that around two thousand people in the small town where I practised were walking round in circles and falling down a good deal. On reflection, I'm surprised some bright spark working at the local hospital didn't diagnose an epidemic of some rare neurological condition. Anyway, I managed to cure the patients of their tendency to walk around in circles by telling them to throw away their inner raises or to have their extra shoe heels removed. Once again I did not want to cast aspersions on my predecessor so I told all the patients that they were now cured.

And there was a third quirk too.

When my predecessor had a disagreement of any kind with a patient he would write 'PSYCHOPATH' on their medical records in blue ink. He wrote in large capital letters so that there could be no mistaking it. Around a fifth of the patients had their medical records envelope decorated in this way. Since patients were usually entrusted with bringing their records into the surgery, they clearly found this embarrassing. I didn't think any of my patients really were psychopaths, certainly not 500 of them, so I tried to help a little by attempting to remove the inscriptions. I tried ink eradicator but it didn't work so I simply cut the tops off the medical records envelopes. The patients concerned, quite a few of whom had responsible jobs in the town, and were also worried because people had noticed that they had a tendency to walk around in circles and to fall over, were quite grateful.

These days I wonder what quirks I might have had and what my successor might have thought of my prescribing habits. I've never had the nerve to try to find out, and I've been retired from practice for so long now that I rather suspect that my immediate successor has himself probably retired by now. And, of course, all my scribbled notes will have doubtless long ago disappeared because all the medical records will have been put into a computer for everyone and his dog to access and peruse whenever they like.

When I was in practice, my cardboard record envelopes were kept in drawers and boxes and my receptionist's filing system was so individual in its design that the records could not have been safer and less accessible if they had been stored in the Bank of England.

I have long been convinced that not all progress is progress as I understand it. But then I suspect that most people would now describe me as an old fogey and long since out of fashion. The medical authorities, who heartily disapprove of experience, long ago decided that I had passed my use-by date. As for my predecessor; well, he would not last five minutes these days.

However, when I think about it, I suspect that making your patients walk round in circles, and fall down, was probably considerably less damaging than some of the things doctors do to their patients these days.

An Old Lady

An old lady whom Antoinette had met in the street came to tea. She had a face that would have served her with distinction had she been a professional mourner in the days when it was customary for the deceased to travel in a carriage drawn by plumed horses.

For no good reason that I could discern, she announced she had recently had a visit from the ghost of her dead husband. Having said this she then looked at me. 'He looked better than you do,' she said. She was just being honest but she might have sugar coated the thought.

Spotting the Bechstein grand piano in our drawing room, she told Antoinette to play something. Antoinette dutifully sat down but had not played more than a handful of notes before the old lady booted her out of the way, sat down and produced a painful cacophony. 'The piano is out of tune,' she said dismissively. She then asked me what I did. I said I wrote books. 'But do you have any talents or skills?' she asked.

I don't think she was being particularly rude. I think it was just something that came naturally.

I said I looked after the garden and was very good at lighting bonfires. (I am particularly proud of the fact that I once had a splendid bonfire in a snowstorm. The trick about bonfires is that they need far more air than they are usually given. I find cardboard boxes and empty plastic bottles an excellent aid to producing a good bonfire. The cardboard box can be used to provide more combustible material with some shelter from rain and snow and the empty plastic bottles provide reserves of oxygen to keep the fire going.)

She then talked a good deal more about herself. We told her about Antoinette's cancer and the treatment she was having at the time.

'Of course, people get cancer because they have done something evil. It is a punishment from God,' she stated, as though this were a fact that was beyond dispute.

At this point I beat her over the head and buried her in the garden. Or, at least, I should have done. Anyway, she won't be coming to tea again.

    When she goes to heaven I fear she will complain bitterly that the harps are out of tune, the clouds are lumpy and that the angels need to stand up straighter.

Donat

'What do I require from life? Just this: the courage to live it to the full; the wisdom to live it memorably.' Robert Donat (1937)

Mrs Caldicot: The Premiere

Antoinette and I were invited to the Royal Premiere of the film of my novel *Mrs Caldicot's Cabbage War*. I can't remember the name of the cinema but it was one of the big ones in Leicester Square. Guests received the full red carpet treatment.

We didn't go. Can you believe that? We didn't go.

It was my fault.

I told myself that it was too far to travel just to go to the cinema, that we would have to fix a hotel, and that I didn't like crowds.

But it wasn't any of that.

We didn't go because they wanted me to pay £15 each for the tickets.

It wasn't meanness. I don't think meanness is one of my many faults.

But I was narked that I was being asked to pay for a ticket to see a film that wouldn't have existed if it had not been for my book.

Childish.

A very small regret but a regret nevertheless.

When I remembered this incident I remembered that when I received the producer's contract for the film, Antoinette and I were staying in a hotel in Devon. The contract came through as a long roll of fax paper. I think there were about eighteen pages in all. I didn't understand any of it and was too stupid and stubborn to consult an entertainment lawyer. I tried to sort through it all by myself and discovered later that I had crossed out most of the clauses which would have brought me most money.

Still I did have one bright idea.

I insisted that when the film was made, my credit as the author of the original book would be the same size as the director's and would remain on screen for the same length of time. I thought it might help sell copies of book. Sadly, it did no good at all because no publisher would publish a mass market edition of the book because the original hardback had been self-published. And when I produced a paperback, bookshops wouldn't stock the book because it was self-published and, therefore, quite unacceptable.

Still, my name was on the big screen long enough for my parents to spot it and point it out to each other. They were prouder of that than of anything else I'd ever done in my life. I pointed out that I could take no credit for the film but that didn't diminish their delight. And the producer sent us a huge hamper of expensive delicacies to celebrate the launch. Movie people do that sort of thing.

Antoinette and I did go to a preview in a screening theatre at Pinewood. We sat with John Alderton who starred in the film with his wife Pauline Collins. Afterwards, I tried unsuccessfully to sell the director the idea of filming the second book in the series (*Mrs Caldicot's Knickerbocker Glory*) but he was a director not a producer and wasn't much interested.

We watched the film later in a cinema in Exeter, and I was moved when the entire audience stood up spontaneously at the end and applauded. I've never seen that happen before though I am told it did happen quite often when the film was shown. (No one knew that Mrs Caldicot's creator was in the audience. Afterwards we stood in the foyer and listened to all the praise for the film. It did me no end of good.)

The film is still shown regularly on British television. I don't give a fig that I signed away most of the royalties to which I was entitled. Someone spent over £12 million turning a little fantasy of mine into something approaching reality.

I did discover one beauty of having a book turned into a film. As the author of the book, I feel quite entitled to accept any praise forthcoming without having to accept any of the criticism. It's one of the few win-win situations in life.

How a Cat Called Alice Changed My Life

A tortoiseshell cat called Alice changed my life in several very important ways. I found her at a cat sanctuary in Stratford-upon-Avon and she came to live with me in 1983. She was loveable from the start but adopted me as her mother when, while trying to use the loo as a human might, she fell into the bowl. I fished her out, dried her with a towel and tucked inside my shirt so that my body warmth would heat her up. She loved me forever after that and hardly left my side.

I have always been opposed to the use of animals in scientific experiments, regarding vivisection as a barbaric and pointless activity. I had written scathingly about researchers of all kinds (including those performing animal experiments) when I wrote my second book, *Paper Doctors*, back in 1976.

I realised one day how lucky I was to have met Alice and how awful it would have been if, instead of coming to live with me, she had somehow found her way into a vivisector's laboratory. The thought of Alice strapped into a harness in a laboratory while a scientist sewed up her eyelids or injected chemicals into her brain was for me a living nightmare. It is not widely realised but vivisectors around the world use thousands of former pets. Thousands of domestic cats and dogs are picked up out of the streets and sold to vivisectors who like using them because they are more trusting and less likely to bite than animals which have not grown up in loving human company. The thought of Alice being kidnapped, sold to a laboratory and used as experimental material was almost too awful to bear.

Ever since my days at medical school I had spent much of my time speaking about vivisection and writing columns and articles about it but gradually, during the 1980s I began to spend even more of my life campaigning for animal rights. That was the first way in which Alice changed my life. I even founded an organisation called Plan 2000 to organise my campaigns – editing and running a small magazine, producing and distributing many thousands of leaflets and booklets, buying display advertising in the national press and, with help from volunteer supporters, collecting support from over 100 A list celebrities all over the world.

It was because I was terrified of Alice and her half-sister, a mackerel tabby called Thomasina, being run over (or, indeed, kidnapped by vivisectors) that I moved to a house in the country – well away from a public road.

In the countryside I spent hours watching lambs playing in the fields and realised that they played just the same sort of games as young children. They play tag, hide and seek and king of the castle. I realised that they, like Alice, had thoughts and emotions and rights. As a city dweller and a scientist, I had never before been exposed to the idea that eating animals might be wrong. My medical training had convinced me (as it convinces most doctors) that eating animals was essential for my very survival and continued good health.

And so it was Alice who led to my giving up eating meat.

It was also Alice who was responsible for my starting to publish my own books.

By the mid-1980s, I felt that I knew Alice well enough to write a book with her. And so together we produced *Alice's Diary – The Memoirs of a Cat*. I had been a professional writer for some years and at the time it was unusual for me to write a book without having found a publisher. My agent usually arranged a contract before I started to write. But this book was different: I felt I had to write it, but since I wasn't quite sure how it was going to turn out I didn't think there was much point in trying to find a publisher to commission it.

When I'd finished the book I felt it needed illustrating. I knew exactly what sort of drawings I wanted but I didn't know an illustrator I could trust to draw Alice and Thomasina. So I did the drawings myself.

When the book and illustrations were finished, the typescript started a long and fruitless journey around London. Publisher after publisher turned it down. They all seemed puzzled by the book and by the fact that I'd written it.

'This isn't the sort of book Vernon usually writes.'
'Is it intended for children or adults?'
'Who is going to buy it?'
'I don't understand it.'

'Vernon doesn't write cat books.'

After a year or two it was clear that no one wanted to publish *Alice's Diary*.

I, however, felt certain that there was a market. So I published it myself. I deliberately didn't put my name on the cover. I gave Alice, my co-author, all the credit.

Within a very short time I had sold over 10,000 hardback copies – big enough sales to have put the book into the bestseller lists for many weeks if we had been a 'proper' publishing company. Despite the misgivings of the professional publishers in London, there clearly were people who wanted to read a book written by a cat. At the time I remember being rather pleasantly surprised that they were all wrong. These days I so expect the 'professionals' to be completely out of touch with what the reading public really wants that I would be worried if I thought I had written a book which any London publisher would want to put on his or her list.

Readers started buying additional copies for friends (I remember that quite early on, one reader ordered eleven copies to give away as presents) and Alice started to receive fan mail.

The next book I published myself was called *Toxic Stress*. I had never had much difficulty in selling medical book ideas to publishers but somehow I knew that this book would never make an orthodox publisher sit up and take notice. I didn't even offer the typescript to any ordinary publishers. The success of *Alice's Diary* had given me confidence and I had discovered that I much enjoyed having total control of the publication process. Without editors or marketing men to interfere, publishing is a real joy.

The Village Cricket Tour – a novel describing the adventures of a cricket team on tour around the West Country – came next. I can't remember why I decided to write that book. It probably just happened. I always have several dozen book ideas jostling for attention and this one just managed to clamber to the front of my brain and demand to be written next. I remember that the initial print run was 5,000 copies, and early on in the book's history most of these were stored in a barn. A visitor, looking at the rather frightening piles of books, asked me if I thought I might have printed too many.

It wasn't long before readers of *Alice's Diary* wanted to know if Alice was going to write another book. And so, in 1992, the same year as *The Village Cricket Tour*, along came *Alice's Adventures*.

In 1994, I wrote a book entitled *Betrayal of Trust* – a considerably extended version of a special report called *Why Doctors Do More Harm than Good* which I had written for the *European Medical Journal*. The report had been published in paperback form in 1993, had been reprinted several times, had sold several thousand copies and had attracted a considerable amount of media attention. In one three day period alone I remember doing around twenty local radio interviews.

Betrayal of Trust was a double edged book. I regarded it primarily as an attack on the medical profession and the pharmaceutical industry (and the dependence of the former on the latter) but also as an animal rights book since it contained the names of dozens of drugs which are sold as suitable for doctors to prescribe for patients but which are known to cause extremely serious problems (such as cancer) when given to animals. I felt then (and still believe) that the book provided the evidence which proved once and for all that animal experiments are of no scientific value, making it crystal clear that drug companies use animal experiments as a double edged tool. If, when a drug is tested on animals, there are no signs of any problems, the drug company will enthusiastically use the experiments as proof that the drug is safe. On the other hand, if the animal tests show that there are problems – for example, because the drug causes cancer, heart disease or kills the animal – the drug company will completely ignore the tests on the grounds that animals are quite different to human beings.

I sent the typescript of *Betrayal of Trust* to just about every publisher I could think of. No one was prepared to publish it. Some said the style was too 'popular'. Other publishers used the excuse that the book was too 'academic'.

I rather suspected that no one wanted to publish the book because they were frightened that it might annoy the medical and scientific establishment too much. They were doubtless also worried that the book might attract lawsuits.

So, with the success of *Alice's Diary* and the other self-publishing ventures behind me, I decided to publish *Betrayal of Trust* myself. I didn't care whether or not it made money. I didn't even mind if it lost money. I just felt that the message it contained was so important that the book had to be published. The commercial and financial success of *Alice's Diary* made it much easier to take this decision, and so once again Alice had affected my life. If I hadn't published *Alice's Diary* I doubt if *Betrayal of Trust* would ever have been published. (In the 'old' days, publishers used to utilise the profits from their bestselling books to subsidise books that they cared about passionately but which they knew would never make much, if any, money.)

I had published *Alice's Diary* and the other fiction books I had written under the Chilton Designs imprint but although I had published *Toxic Stress* under this imprint I didn't feel that *Betrayal of Trust* would fit comfortably alongside a growing collection of novels and the first one or two of a series of books set in a Devon village called Bilbury.

I was already publishing a quarterly medical journal which I had founded a year or two earlier (and which was circulating throughout the world in both English and German, but far from breaking even financially) and the publication was called the *European Medical Journal* and so I decided to publish *Betrayal of Trust* as a *European Medical Journal* book.

Much to my surprise, the hardback of *Betrayal of Trust* sold over 12,000 copies and a paperback did well.

(Early on in my career as a publisher, I approached a solicitor and asked him to try to arrange for the *European Medical Journal* and the associated book publishing operation to be turned into a proper charity. Knowing that I could live on the income from the columns I was writing, I even planned to donate all my other book royalties to the charity in order to give it a constant income. To my disappointment I discovered that I could not turn EMJ Books into a charity. The main problem was the fact that the publishing programme was regarded as having 'campaigning' overtones. The fact that I couldn't run the EMJ publishing operation as a charity (together with the fact that unexpected and heavy legal expenses led to the closing of the *European Medical Journal*) resulted in my decision to take personal financial responsibility for all the EMJ Books I was planning to publish and to bring them within my general publishing activities.)

The first commercially successful book which I published under the EMJ imprint was *Food for Thought*, a book which had originally been written as part of a series of books I had agreed to write for one of the world's largest publishers.

The publishers and I disagreed about the content of *Food for Thought*. They felt that the book was too controversial, too opinionated and contained too much of an attack on meat. They wanted me to change the text. I disagreed with them and wanted to keep the book as it was. In the end I asked them if I could keep the book and abandon the contract. They agreed.

Since then *Food for Thought* has, despite being a campaigning book, proved to be a huge commercial success. It reprinted five times in the first twelve months and was our first official 'bestseller'. Numerous foreign publishers bought the rights and the book became the financial backbone of the EMJ Books imprint.

When I was a boy I frequently read with admiration about the relationship between authors and publishers. An author and a publisher would stay together for life in what was more like a marriage than a commercial partnership.

But, sadly, by the time I started writing books, the world of publishing had changed irrevocably.

The first big change was that editors started moving about between publishing houses. Authors found themselves having a book commissioned by one enthusiastic editor and aided through the editorial production process by a second editor. The book would then be brought into the world by a third editor who might, or might not, like the author or his work. The old-fashioned, cosy relationship between publisher and author had changed for ever.

The second big change was that salesmen and marketing directors had taken over the world of publishing. It seems to me that editors no longer had control over which books they would publish. The traditional publishing image of a wise, well-read man in a tweed jacket helping an author to turn his raw pages into a good book – and then helping to create an oeuvre – had been out of date for decades. Publishing, I realised, was controlled by marketing men in smart suits. The marketing men (and women) wanted more of what was already selling and they panicked when they realised that the market was saturated with too much of the same.

To my astonishment, I learned that the marketing men were telling editors what to commission. The editors then had to find an author and tell him to write a book he doesn't particularly want to write. The result, inevitably, was a good many books written without passion which failed to excite readers.

I'd also found that most of the people in the publishing industry were scared stiff by the very thought of innovation. They preferred to imitate.

The great beauty of having my own publishing company was that I could write the books I want to write – and then worry later about how to sell them.

Many of the books I have chosen to write in recent years would not have been published by a modem publishing conglomerate. And yet most of the books I have chosen to write and publish have been reprinted (some of them many times) and have sold well. Many of the books would have been on the best-seller lists if they had been sold more through the bookshops (where the official best-seller lists are created) and less through the post direct to readers.

I can still remember that when I used to write for big well-known publishers, just about every book I ever published involved a battle. Editors, sometimes hardly into their twenties, had very certain ideas on how I should write a book, what it should contain and so on.

So, for example, it took years to find someone brave enough to publish my book *Bodypower* – an account of the human body's many protective mechanisms. Publisher after publisher insisted that there was no market for such a book. And yet *Bodypower* went straight into the *Sunday Times* bestseller top ten and has never been out of print since. It has been translated into over a dozen languages, and extracts from it have appeared in scores of newspapers and magazines around the world. I have made several television series and a radio series based on it.

When the original paperback version of *Bodypower* went out of print, a mass market paperback house bought the rights. Their edition went out of print before it was even published. I took the rights back and sold the book to another publisher. When they, in turn, remaindered their version, I bought up all their stock (around 2,000 copies), gave them away (because they had cut some material out of the book) and published my own *European Medical Journal* version.

Today, over 40 years after it was first published, *Bodypower* still sells several thousand copies a year in the English edition alone. British readers of *The Good Book Guide* voted it one of their 100 favourite books of all time.

When I first wanted to write a book about tranquilliser addiction, just about every publisher in London told my agent that there was no market for such a book. When a publisher eventually commissioned *Life Without Tranquillisers*, they wanted major changes making to the book I produced. I refused to make the changes, and so my agent at the time took the book away and sold it to another publisher. The book went straight into *The Sunday Times Top Ten* the minute it came out. I remember that someone at the publishers rang the *Sunday Times* to find out why the book had gone into the bestseller list. 'Because it is selling so quickly,' was the logical reply.

I could fill a book with stories like this.

Over the years, after I started publishing my books myself, I was approached by a number of literary agents in other countries. They then sold my books in translated versions. For example, one publisher in Portugal produced versions of 15 of my books. Agents in the United States, Germany, China, Russia and many other countries sold my self-published books in their countries.

I found that I could publish books in a tenth of the time taken by publishers in London. And I found that I was prepared to take risks with books that established publishers would be too frightened to put their names to.

The one surmountable problem I had was that I found it nigh on impossible to persuade small bookshops to take my books. I offered a very good discount and paid to have the books posted to the bookshops. In addition, I agreed to take back any book which a bookshop ordered but couldn't sell. This meant that bookshops took no risk and had absolutely nothing to lose. I supported this by spending a fortune on advertising my books in the national press. Bookshops could order my books without any risk whatsoever.

Despite all this, bookshops were extremely unwilling to take my books unless they had been ordered specifically by a customer.

I remember one bookshop once telephoned on a Monday to order a copy of *Alice's Diary* for a customer. A member of the Publishing House staff accepted the order (on credit) and posted the book. (I obviously needed a good deal of help to run what had become a decent sized publishing company. At one point I had 15 members of staff.) On the following day, the bookshop rang again and ordered another copy of the same book. We accepted their order and posted a second book. On the Wednesday they rang again. This time they had two orders for *Alice's Diary*. We posted them two books. When they rang on the Thursday to order another copy we asked if they would like to take a few copies on sale or return. We said that this would enable them to have a better discount, it would mean that they would be able to supply their customers immediately and, if they put the books on their shelves, it might mean that they would sell a few additional copies. They said that they did not think that this was a good idea and that they would continue to order books as customers asked for them.

Even more frustrating were those bookshops where the staff insisted that my books simply did not exist. My staff regularly took telephone calls from would-be purchasers who reported that they had visited every bookshop for miles around and been told that *Alice's Diary* (or whatever other title they are asking for) did not exist. All my books were listed on computers, microfiche and in every reference book, and were available from the major wholesalers, but there were bookshops which still insisted that my books didn't exist.

I ran my publishing imprints rather in the way that I believe old-fashioned publishers used to operate. I wrote books which I wanted to write (rather than books which I knew would be commercially successful). Only when the book was written did I worry about how to sell it. And at the end of the financial year, I hoped that the books which sold well would earn enough to subsidise the books for which there is not such a clear market.

I believe that there are only three reasons to do anything: to try to change the world, to have fun and to make money. Sometimes it is possible to do things which satisfy all these three objectives. More often the success of one objective means that one is more capable of pursuing another objective. So, for example, making money doing something which is dull may enable you to enjoy an experience which is fun.

But only very occasionally is it really possible to combine all three of these reasons. And I may be kidding myself but I believe that many of the books which I wrote and published myself satisfied all three objectives.

Alice changed my life but she didn't have things all her own way.

Stocks of *Alice's Diary* and *Alice's Adventures* were both stored in a barn for some years. When I moved the stock to a new and larger warehouse, I discovered that mice had eaten the covers and spines of some of the books.

Alice would have been furious if she had known.

After Alice died, I buried her with a copy of *Alice's Diary* and her favourite jumper of mine. (It was my favourite jumper too). I buried her in a wooden casket with a proper granite headstone, with her name and dates carved in it.

And I had the details and position of her grave written into the house deeds so that if anyone ever tried to disturb her resting place the ownership of the house would revert to my estate. The lawyer who drew up the codicil assured me that it was legally unbreakable.

Note: A different version of this essay was first published as an Extra in my book *Alice and Other Friends*.

George and Millie

For twenty years Antoinette and I had an apartment in Paris. We had the whole top floor of a 19th century building no more than a three wood shot from the Champs de Mars and the Eiffel Tower. We were within easy walking distance of six good supermarkets, four excellent bakeries, three shops selling wine, two picture framers, more hairdressers and beauty salons than I could count and enough restaurants to be able to eat at a different one every day for a month. In Paris, in those days, the council used to encourage small shopkeepers to stay in business by making sure that the taxes they paid weren't too high. In our street we even had a specialist curtain shop and a shop run by a man who stuffed mattresses to order. In the next street there was a shop selling nothing but vacuum cleaners, another selling refrigerators and a third selling safes.

We also had the American Library just a few minutes' walk away. Almost every day the library would put out a rack containing books which they no longer required and which they were giving away free of charge. I always found something worth reading and, over the years, found a number of authors whose work wasn't published in England. Latterly, however, the Library stopped this practice. There were a number of attacks on American addresses and I think the librarians were frightened that someone might put a bomb onto the book rack, timed to go off after they'd wheeled it back into the library in the late afternoon.

We eventually sold the apartment, which we had owned for over two decades, with considerable reluctance. We sold it for several reasons.

First, the building where we lived was originally occupied almost entirely by old people who were always polite and genteel and whom we saw most days as they wandered out to do their daily shopping. As they died, so their apartments were sold to investors and property companies who let out the properties to tenants who didn't give a damn about the building. They threw their rubbish out of the windows and left the hall, staircase and lift dirty. They broke things (such as the lift), had noisy all night parties and crammed large amounts of people into tiny apartments.

Second, since we owned the whole top floor of the building, our share of the maintenance costs were high. The agents hired to look after the building were rude and unhelpful and so arrogant that they ignored the annual vote of the owners. We found that we were paying for the decisions made by a couple of snooty 25-year-old Anglophobic Parisians. We eventually began to suspect that they were having work done simply for the commissions they were being paid by the builders they hired.

Third, when a cable company dug up the pavement outside the building, the workmen also dug underneath all the buildings in the street. When they had finished, they filled the holes they'd made underneath the building but instead of using something solid they used sand. Not surprisingly, within months huge cracks started to appear in the huge, thick walls of the building. I suspect that if our building hadn't been held up by all the other buildings in the street, it would have fallen down – as, indeed, would all the other buildings, collapsing like a row of dominos. The building had been standing for a century and a half. I doubt if it will last another ten years.

Fourth, the politicians running Paris decided that they didn't like foreigners bringing money into the city. Taxes were put up for people not born in France. New rules were introduced to regulate foreigners but not locals. We were deliberately made to feel unwelcome. I hate to stay where I know I'm not wanted. The political rhetoric began to filter through to ordinary Parisians, making life unpleasant.

Fifth, French workmen (possibly encouraged by the xenophobic politicians running Paris) became increasingly difficult and even more unreliable than they had been before.

Sixth, travel to and from France became a nightmare. When we first bought the apartment we used to go to France every two weeks (except in the summer when most of Paris shuts and the heat becomes unbearable). We did this for several years, splitting our time between France and the UK. We travelled on Eurostar. But gradually travel became increasingly tiresome. First, the customs regulations got tougher. It took a long time to get through the formalities. Then the trains were modernised and became uncomfortable and unpleasant. Travel within the UK became unbearable too. In the beginning we could drive from our home to the Eurostar station in Ashford in three or four hours. By the time we gave up, it was taking twice that long. Endless, inexplicable delays on the motorways made it difficult to rely on arriving at the station unless we set off many hours before we were due to travel.

Seventh, Paris changed. At the end of the 20th century our arrondissement was like a village. The staff in the supermarket used to greet us with a handshake and a ca va? The man in the newspaper kiosk greeted us with a cheery smile. Waiters in our favourite café used to rush to shake hands. Twenty years later all this had gone. Changes in local taxation policies meant that many of the small shops had to shut and were turned into small apartments. Within one six month period, in our street alone, we lost both picture framers, the mattress maker, the woman who made curtains and blinds, the man who did nothing but polish shoes, the ironmonger and so on and so on.

But we still miss the apartment and we are left with some extraordinary memories.

We didn't know many people in Paris. We kept largely to ourselves. In the evenings we listened to music, played games and read. But we did meet one or two interesting folk who became rather more than acquaintances but, perhaps, not quite friends.

So, for example, there were Millie and George.

Millie was a rich, Canadian who wrote a newsletter about finance, geopolitics and investments and had been doing it for years before the word 'geopolitics' had become widely known or understood. She was, I guessed, in her 70s and quite deaf but refused to use a hearing aid. Instead of a hearing aid she carried an old-fashioned ear trumpet and shouted a good deal. She didn't suffer fools gladly and didn't put up with anything else she didn't like. We once took the two of them for a meal at the Hard Rock café in Paris (they usually ate in one of the big hotels so this was something of an adventure for them) and Millie complained to the waiter that the music was so loud that she couldn't hear anything we were saying to her. So pungent was her demand that the volume be turned down that the manager did just that – turned the music right down so that it could hardly be heard. I have to admit that the other customers didn't seem to mind.

Neither Millie nor George had ever bothered to learn to speak French though occasionally George could be heard to mutter 'mercy buckets' to a particularly attentive waiter or porter at the Ritz Hotel in the Place Vendome, where they lived in a huge, permanent suite. I hate to think what the suite cost them but they liked it because they never had to worry about utility bills, laundry or replacing spent light-bulbs.

We met them one evening in the Restaurant Drouot, in the Rue de Richelieu. We were there because it was a traditional Parisian restaurant which served excellent, cheap food. (I think it has gone now, though I dread to think what has replaced it.) I remember that the table cloths were made of paper, a fairly common occurrence in French restaurants patronised by the French. I liked them for their doodling qualities but Millie and George thought them a little down market for their taste.

George and Millie were there because they occasionally liked to venture outside their comfort zone (the Ritz dining room) and sample what they called 'quaint Paris eateries'. They usually preferred to eat at restaurants where the menu was written in English except for the bits of it which read a l'Americaine. Millie once confessed that they felt happier in restaurants where at least 50% of the clientele had been born in the United States of America.

Their problem was that they didn't speak a word of French and the waiters at Drouot, not being accustomed to English speaking customers, either didn't speak a word of their language or pretended that they didn't. They were sat at the table next to us, and after we had helped them navigate the menu, they insisted on taking us for coffee and after dinner drinks at the Café de la Paix in front of L'Opera. (The bill for the coffee and after dinner drinks came to considerably more than the bill for excellent three course meals for four people at Drouot.

They were unlike any couple we'd ever met before and I think we were unlike any couple they'd ever met. So, the four of us hit it off quite well and by the evening a friendship was beginning to develop.

Millie didn't think that anyone would buy a newsletter about finance and geopolitics if it was written by a woman so she wrote and edited it under a nom de plume – she called herself Arthur Finghorn. She reckoned that no one would imagine that anyone would call themselves Arthur Finghorn if that were not their real name.

Most of her subscribers were American, British or German and most of them were also millionaires with an aversion to paying too much tax. She charged them $1,000 a year for the newsletter, which was little more than a flimsy, twelve-page leaflet published six times a year. 'If you charge a good deal for something,' explained Millie, 'people will think it's really worth having. If I charged £100 a year, no one would think my newsletter anything special.' The high fee also meant that Millie could be confident that all her customers were on the rich side of wealthy and therefore suitable targets for the other services which she and George offered.

Her husband, George, a diminutive, rather mousy looking fellow, ran an entirely separate but connected business. He sold high risk investment advice and, like his wife, he charged huge fees for his opinions. He always pointed out to his clients that his fees were tax deductible and, therefore, not quite as painful as they might otherwise have been.

Although he offered advice to Millie's customers, George shamelessly gathered clients with a variation on an old trick long favoured by tricksters selling race course tips. He used to put advertisements in smart newspapers and magazines (the sort offering advertisements for holidays in the Seychelles and high end motor cars). He targeted potential clients who were prepared to take a risk with some of their money in the hope of making a 'killing'. He told us that in the investment business, a share whose price increases ten-fold is known as a 'ten bagger' but was, he added, worth far more than to his clients who would be able to brag about their gains at their club.

George would offer to send enquirers who wrote in, an entirely free investment tip and he always had six potential share tips ready and waiting. The companies he selected were small and invariably operating in areas where companies sometimes went bust and sometimes did incredibly well. So, for example, he picked small mining or oil companies, small software companies and small companies with a single new, exciting product to sell.

He would divide up his tips among the people who wrote in. If an advertisement drew in 1,000 replies, he would divide up the names and send each of his share tips to around 175 of the people who wrote in.

Most of the time, one or two of the tips would prove profitable – sometimes very profitable. And this usually happened very quickly.

The others, of course, would either do nothing or would head down on the slippery slope to bankruptcy.

George would write to the correspondents whose tip had done well and he would draw attention to the profit they had enjoyed – or would have enjoyed if they'd followed his tip! He would then invite them to subscribe to his tip sheet – for which he charged £1,500 for a year's subscription, to be paid with a credit card. (Most subscribers who pay by credit card never bother to cancel a subscription.) His 'selling' letter was well written and at least a fifth would subscribe, more than covering all his costs to date.

Each tip sheet, sent by fax once a month, would contain at least six recommendations – all selected for their potential to go up or down dramatically. The ones which failed would be quietly forgotten and never mentioned again. But the ones which succeeded would be referred to constantly, both in the tip sheet itself and in future advertisements.

(Years later this system was still popular with racing tipsters operating newspaper or telephone tipping services. The scam is so old that I wouldn't be surprised to hear that some Stone Age man used it to sell details of the best hunting grounds to his neighbours.)

The fees Millie and George charged were only part of their income and merely the hors d'oeuvre to some very fancy schemes which had made the pair very rich.

So, for example, they offered a service which charged massive fees for consultations on a wide range of topics. The customer (invariably a rich individual with an aversion to paying too much tax) would pay over $100,000 for 'consultancy' work (and receive a properly receipted invoice in return for their accounts). Millie and George would deduct $15,000 as their 'real' fee and then put the remainder into an offshore bank account in the customer's name.

For the customer this was a profitable exercise. The $100,000 fee could be deducted as a genuine business expense, and $85,000 would go into the offshore account – usually a numbered account in Switzerland.

Occasionally, the sums of money that would need to be transferred would be too liquid to be moved in this way. A millionaire with a large undeclared cash income would turn up at the Ritz in Paris with a gold nugget, a small white envelope full of diamonds or a few very rare and expensive postage stamps which had been purchased in their home country – usually the USA. Postage stamps, Millie once told me, are the favoured way of moving large sums of money around without anyone taking any notice. And the dealers' turn, at both ends of the transaction, takes only a relatively small bite out of the sum involved.

Millie and George would then sell the gold nugget, the diamonds or the stamps to an appropriate dealer in Paris, take their usual 15%, and put the remaining cash into a 'black' numbered account. The selling costs, together with the 15% charged by Millie and George, were what they called the 'overhead'. Millie claimed that having to pay outrageous fees for the privilege of cheating the taxman made many of their investors feel better about themselves. She said that being scammed themselves made them feel less guilty about scamming the Government.

George told me that their customers liked the fact that their money was tucked away offshore in a hidden and private account. It seemed exciting, rather romantic indeed; especially since they knew that when the 'hidden' money was invested there would be no future tax liabilities on any future profits. Naturally, Millie and George, who had shared access to the numbered account, would take a small but noticeable annual fee for managing their client's investments.

George was an accomplished and successful trader who specialised in commodity trading. He sat staring at half a dozen computer screens for eight or ten hours a day and consistently succeeded in making money for himself and his favoured clients.

The pair's greatest achievement, however, was in introducing rich foreigners to the unique joys of the viager system in France. In order to explain what they did I have to explain the bare bones of the viager system. If you know all about it you can skip the next few paragraphs.

The French viager scheme is a tiny bit like the system of equity release that is now so common in countries such as the UK. Equity release schemes enable home owners to release some of the capital from their property while being allowed to remain in their home until they die. The equity release system doubtless helps some elderly folk, especially those who aren't interested in leaving anything to relatives, friends or charities, but the effective rate of interest is pretty savage.

The idea of the viager system, on the other hand, is that instead of lending money against a property an old person owns, the purchaser buys a property that has someone living in it, but allows the seller to stay in their home as long as they are around. The buyer won't be able to take possession until the seller has died.

For everyone concerned, it's all a huge gamble, though the person with most to lose is, of course, the purchaser, who has no idea when they will be able to take possession of the property they have bought because that depends on the longevity of the seller. The seller, meanwhile, has all the cash from the sale of their home while retaining the right to live in the property which they no longer own. Most sellers are widowers or widows but occasionally an elderly couple will sell their home this way. When that happens it is called 'un viager sur deux tetes' and the buyer cannot take possession of the property until both the sellers are safely tucked up in their chosen cemetery.

The price the buyer has to pay will depend to a great extent upon the age and health of the seller. So, if the seller is aged 65 and as fit as a flea, the purchaser will pay much less than if the seller is aged 95 and in poor health. Odd things sometimes happen with this system. So, for example, a woman called Jeanne Calment, who lived to be 122, and was the world's oldest woman at the time, comfortably outlived the person who had 'bought' her apartment.

The rule is that for a viager contract to be legal, the death of the seller must be unpredictable. So the buyer cannot have inside knowledge of the seller's state of health. This rule means that doctors, lawyers and relatives are (legally, at least) prevented from taking advantage of anything they know about the property's owner. If this rule didn't exist, doctors would be able to make a killing by buying up flats and houses belonging to terminally ill patients.

The price the buyer pays is a percentage of the market value. The percentage obviously varies with the age of the seller but it is usually around 30% of the estimated value. This sum is called the 'bouquet'. But this isn't all the buyer has to pay. In addition to the 'bouquet', the buyer has to pay the seller a regular monthly or quarterly 'rent viager'.

Foreigners sometimes find it difficult to accept that, having bought a property they not only have to pay the seller a fixed sum but also have to pay them rent while they continue to live there. To Anglo Saxon minds it all seems a little topsy turvy, not to say complete barking.

And just to make things more complicated, there is actually a variation on the viager scheme.

The usual type of viager is called viager occupe because, as I've explained, the seller remains in their home. There is a variation called viager libre in which the seller moves out but the buyer pays them a rent for their lifetime (to cover their living costs in the nursing home or hotel to which they have moved). Millie and George didn't usually bother with buying a property this way because it added an extra layer of complication to something that was already complicated enough.

Naturally, not every buyer is happy to wait indefinitely for their seller to complete the agreement by dying, and as I write this there are two murder cases in the French courts which involve buyers who have been charged with killing tenants in order to obtain possession of viager properties more speedily than God had intended. I'm sure that Millie and George would have never considered anything so crude. They were quite capable of making good money without taking such risks.

Some of Millie's and George's clients were naturally cautious about investing in a scheme which seemed so potentially risky, and it was George who found a way of encouraging rich people to take a gamble and invest their money in a viager – a piece of property which they would not be able to occupy or use until someone unknown to them had died and to whom, moreover, they would have had to pay a regular rent for the rest of their lifetime.

Even Millie and George agreed that viagers were not the most obviously attractive investments. However, they were keen on selling them because they received hefty fees from the estate agent, from the notaire representing the seller and from their rich purchaser. Three commissions on a single transaction was simply too tempting to be ignored.

The key, when purchasing a viager, lies in estimating just how long the seller is likely to remain alive and in residence. And (technically at least) the purchaser is not allowed to cheat. Asking the seller if they have any serious illnesses is strictly taboo, as is endeavouring to obtain such information from a relative or doctor. It is considered to be the equivalent of nobbling a horse, playing with loaded dice or cheating at cards. The authorities take a dimmer view of the buyer who attempts to cheat when buying a viager than they would of the gambler who slips a stable lad a few quid to give a horse an extra bucket of water before a big race.

'What if the seller lives another 20 years?' was the constant query from potential buyers who were themselves usually well into their 60s or 70s.

'Oh, I don't think that's very likely,' Millie would say with her own personal version of a nudge and a wink. 'You take a good look round when we take you to see the apartment this afternoon.'

When the potential buyer, the estate agent and Millie and George arrived at the apartment the aim was partly to check out the general state of the apartment and the building of which it was a part, but also to check out the condition of the owner (or the two owners if the apartment was jointly owned by an elderly couple).

Having previously been advised by George or Millie, the owner would be sitting in an easy chair and would stay there, seemingly too weak to get up and greet the visitors. The owner's lungs would appear to be searching for oxygen and the owner's brain would appear to be a little on the slow side. An open, half empty bottle of wine would be on the table, together with an overflowing ashtray, a couple of packets of Gauloises or Gitanes cigarettes, and a book of matches. One or two cigarettes, perched on the edge of the ashtray, would be smouldering, sending up spirals of smoke. A cardboard box, underneath the table, would be full of empty wine and brandy bottles and the air would be thick enough to chop into cubes.

'Well, she doesn't look as if she's going to last more than a few months!' the buyer would say, as the quartet hit the pavement and headed for the nearest café to discuss the potential purchase. 'Did you see all those bottles? Did you see that ashtray? Unfiltered cigarettes too! I could hardly breathe in there. I think I'd get lung cancer just from spending twenty minutes breathing in that air!'

The buyer would, of course, be unaware that George had, with the connivance of the seller and the estate agent, carefully dressed the 'set' an hour beforehand. The seller, who did not smoke and never drank more than an occasional glass of wine with a meal, would hand the props back to George when he called for them later that evening.

Convinced that he was about to make the killing of a lifetime, and be the possessor of a vacant apartment before he landed back in the

United States, the enthusiastic buyer, straining at the leash and with the cap off his pen in eagerness, would sign the contract that the estate agent had brought with him and leave the meeting so delighted with his purchase that he'd insist on Millie and George finding him another equally attractive bargain while he was in France. The money used to purchase the property was, quite often, money that had been paid to George in 'consultancy' fees.

And George and Millie would collect their fees.

Millie and George did very well with their sales of viager properties.

George told me that he thought they must have arranged forty or fifty such purchases. They were so keen on the whole idea they even bought an apartment themselves; a rather airy, well positioned piece of real estate no more than a couple of hundred yards from the Eiffel Tower. Naturally, however, they made a few cautious enquiries before signing their contract. ('Oh Madame F. is very poorly these days,' confided the concierge. 'She hardly ever leaves her apartment except to go to the hospital for her appointment with the specialist.')

It was a lucky purchase in more ways than one.

Madame F died of heart disease just seven months after she'd sold her apartment, and Millie and George found themselves the owners of a prime piece of Parisian real estate, having paid a third of the market value. They remained at the Ritz for a year or two but rented the apartment to their own subscribers and customers. Naturally, they never failed to tell visitors how they had bought the apartment at a knockdown price.

When we last saw them they had abandoned their suite at the Ritz and were living very quietly in their apartment.

George had retired but Millie was still writing and publishing her newsletter and the two of them were still busy finding investors who were prepared to invest their savings in a French property.

'We can fix you up with a beautiful Parisian apartment, close to the Opera, for a third of its value,' they'd murmur.

And who could resist such an offer?

They'd have died of shame if anyone had accused them of being hustlers, but that's what they both were: natural hustlers.

We both liked them. They were an entertaining couple. I sometimes wish I'd bought a viager property myself. But I never quite had the courage to take the risk. Maybe I've backed too many favourites which have limped in last.

George and Millie have both gone now; but they're probably selling prime cloud space to unsuspecting newcomers.

I could never feel indignant about the viager scam the pair ran because their scheme meant that the old folk selling their homes always got a better deal than they might otherwise have expected. The only losers were the rich people who probably paid a little too much for the properties they bought.

The Scary Phone Box

Horror films were far less scary in the 1960s than they are today. For one thing film companies such as Hammer Films aimed to entertain their customers rather than scare them half to death. And for another, audiences were not as hardened then as they are today. Actors such as Boris Karloff, Vincent Price and Christopher Lee hammed up the horror, with Price in particular usually making it pretty clear that he was playing everything for laughs. I still think that one of the funniest horror movies of all time was Roger Corman's version of *The Raven*, which starred Boris Karloff, Vincent Price, Peter Lorre and a young Jack Nicholson.

Male actors always took the lead roles in the early horror films, with women usually being employed either as innocent maidens in peril or as vampires. The innocent maidens always covered up modestly and the vampires always showed lots of cleavage. It was the way it was.

There is no little irony in the fact that today's young cinema goers are so immune to horror that modern directors need to provide scary scenes that would, in the 1960s, have resulted in half the audience members being carried out of the cinema on stretchers. It's odd that the young are insensitive to horror but apparently so sensitive to ideas that they must be protected from history and from scientific truths which they find unacceptable. Still, that's all by the by and nothing to do with this tale.

One of the scariest films I ever saw back then was something called *The Devil Rides Out*. The film, made by Hammer Films, was based on a book by the accomplished and prolific, but now comparatively forgotten, Denis Wheatley. The star was Christopher Lee who played the Duke de Richleau (one of Wheatley's perennial good guys against the forces of evil). Patrick Mower and Nike Arrighi were the innocent hero and heroine and Charles Gray was the baddie and leader of a devil worshiping group. Mr Lee often said it was the favourite of his own films.

The story, like so much of Wheatley's work, was a tale of black magic, pentagrams and evil spirits conjured up from the spiritual darkness. Cinema patrons were treated to the Goat of Mendes and the Angel of Death (a pretty ripe double act).

Today, I suspect that the film would provoke nothing but laughter and derision but when it came out it was the most frightening film since Nosferatu. Mr Gray was blood chillingly scary and there were some wonderful visual effects of diaphanous beasts arriving from the dark side. The special effects were enough to send shivers up and down anyone's spine. I haven't seen the film for over half a century but I remember that to stay safe our hero and heroine had to stay within the safety of a pentagram drawn on the floor.

I was at medical school when the film came out, sharing a huge rambling flat in a Victorian house in Richmond Hill Road with a couple of other medical students. Our one weekly treat was a visit to a local flea pit of a cinema which specialised in showing B movies, usually horror films, which didn't merit a showing in Birmingham's big cinemas. The films were usually shown as a double bill.

Choc ices, popcorn and orange squash in waxed cartons were served at half time by an ancient soul held together by wrinkles and hope. I remember she had to start her trudge down the central aisle at least twenty minutes before the intermission was due to start, and it took her twenty minutes to trudge back up the aisle after the end of the intermission. Her elastic stockings toyed with gravity long before Nora Batty from *The Last of the Summer Wine* fought the same losing battle.

In retrospect, that ancient cinema reminds me of the crumbling cinema inherited by Virginia McKenna and Bill Travers in *The Smallest Show on Earth*. The only thing missing was Peter Sellers as the projectionist. The building, once exquisitely decorated in gold leaf and red velvet, appeared to be held together only by strands of dry rot and the traditional armies of woodworm holding hands. Much to our disappointment it was knocked down before I qualified. The land has since then been used as, in no particular order, an insurance building, a multi-storey car park and a block of flats.

The day after we had watched the film *The Devil Rides Out* I had to go to London. I can't remember why but it was probably to see a book, magazine or newspaper editor. I didn't do much TV or radio in those days. And at some point I found myself in Knightsbridge waiting to use a phone box opposite Harrods.

I was waiting because the phone box was occupied by a large man in the sort of long shorts Englishmen used to wear on holiday, and a gaudy Hawaiian shirt. I stood patiently outside the box waiting for him to finish. He was facing into the telephone box so I couldn't see his face.

Suddenly, he finished his call, replaced the receiver, turned and flung open the phone box door. The call must have gone well for he emerged from the telephone box, looking straight at me, with a huge, cheek splitting grin on his face.

The man in the unlikely costume was Charles Gray, the actor, the bad egg from the film *The Devil Rides Out* which I had watched the previous evening.

Never before, and never since, have I been so immediately and so thoroughly terrified. Not even the strange costume lessened the sense of shock.

He had to be somewhere, I suppose. We all have to be somewhere.

But did he have to come out of that phone box on the day after I watched *The Devil Rides Out*?

Fifty years on and I can still remember it as though it were yesterday.

Helping Out a Friend

When I first arrived at medical school we all had to live in a Hall of Residence for our first year. I think this was probably to try and stop us all going wild and behaving like medical students.

In my first year I had three close friends. Two of them lived in the same soulless hall of residence where I lived and the third lived in a hall of residence that had character.

Most of the university's halls were, like the one where I lived, modern, purpose built and ghastly. They looked as if they'd been designed and built by architects who were refugees from East Germany. But the hall of residence where my other chum lived was a very different kettle of fish, being a large Victorian mansion which had been converted into what seemed more like a gentleman's club than a doss house for students. There was a snooker room, a decent dining room and an elegantly furnished and well-stocked bar.

Somehow, our chum had succeeded in becoming treasurer of the bar. This sounded a rather dull job but it was a much sought post after because local wine merchants used to send him bottles of wine hoping that he would order a couple of cases for the bar. In that respect it rather reminded me of the sort of appointment PG.Wodehouse's character Bertie Wooster always sought, sadly without success, at the Drones Club.

At the end of our first year, the three of us living in the building put together by East German refugees had a telephone message from our chum in the Victorian Mansion. (When I say we received a telephone message I mean just that. There was a small bank of public phones on the ground floor of our 16 storey East German designed tower block. Most of the time, the phones were occupied with calls going out. Occasionally, however, a phone would be free and it would ring. Someone standing nearby might then answer it, take a message and deliver it. Or they might not.

When we finally got in touch with him, our pal whom I will call Tom (because that wasn't his name and he later became a very eminent surgeon) reported that, having come to the end of the bar's accounting year, he didn't know how to value the bar's remaining stock of half opened spirits. It was, he explained, easy enough to put a value on full bottles of whisky, gin, brandy and so on but how was he supposed to value half a bottle of Rum, a third of a bottle of Gordon's gin, three quarters of a bottle of Laphroaig or an inch or two of liquid in the bottle of a bottle of Corvoisier?

'I have decided,' he announced, 'that the only sensible thing to do is to get rid of all the opened bottles. We can't just leave them where they are because the stuff will go off or decay or turn toxic or something. And it would clearly be a criminal waste to dump the stuff down the sink.'

It was generally agreed by the four of us, without any scientific evidence being offered or considered necessary, that spirits in opened bottles can be as dangerous as opened bottles of medicine if left to deteriorate.

Tom had, therefore, decided that he would drink the stuff. And since there was too much for one, and most of the other residents of his hall of residence had already gone home for the summer holidays, he had rung us to go round and help. (Medical students in those days always had much shorter holidays than students of say, modern languages or mechanical engineering. Tom was the only medical student in his hall of residence and, therefore, the only student there.)

If an excuse is required for what followed (and I am not inclined, as a matter of course, to consider explanations or excuses necessary, wise or inevitability) then I would point out that we were emotionally, physically and mentally exhausted. At the start of the year none of us had much contact with death. But we had spent eight months dissecting cadavers soaked in formalin. We had dissected out every nerve, every artery, every vein, every bone and every organ. We stank of death and dreamt of lists of anatomical structures. We were ripe for some escape.

And so, full of the milk of human kindness, we tottered off to help our chum complete his stock-taking chore. I will refer to my chums as Dick and Harry since those were not their names, and one became an eminent radiologist and the other ended up as an eminent anaesthetist.

There was a lot of booze.

Even for four, fairly large, reasonably healthy medical students there was a good deal of alcohol to get rid of.

We sat and drank for a while, creating some unusual cocktails, as we did so. Then after an hour and a half or so we decided we needed a break. So we tottered out to the local fish and chip shop for bags of heavily battered cod and chip shop chips smothered in gallons of vinegar and pounds of salt. It might be said, without argument that we weren't too hot on nutritional values in those days.

And then it was back to work.

(I should, at some point, and this is as good a point as any, make it clear that this is not something anyone should try at home. It was irresponsible. Moreover, the four protagonists in this true tale were all white and all male. If this episode were ever filmed, at least three of us would have to be ethnic in some way and two would have to be of the feminine gender. But I'm telling it the way it was.)

After another two hours of steady, determined drinking we emptied our wallets and raised enough cash for a visit to the local Chinese takeaway. We were hearty eaters and at six foot three inches tall I was by no means the largest of our quartet. Dick and Harry were both considerably taller and Dick was much more generously built in girth. We had a good deal of space to keep filled.

We ate the Chinese takeaway on the hoof and then it was back to the bar to complete our good turn for the evening.

When, at something after three in the morning, we had finished our work, we said good night to Tom who had collected together all the empty bottles and, in a fit of contrition, was wondering where best to hide them, and headed back to our own hall of residence. Dick, the only one of our quartet who had a motor car, insisted on attempting to drive himself back to our hall of residence and would not be dissuaded from this action. I seem to remember thinking that it was a good thing that the roads were deserted and wondering why this could be. Fortunately, after failing to find any forward gears, Dick abandoned his car and was surprised, later the following day, to find it conveniently parked in a bed of roses which were, thankfully, a couple of months past their prime and which had been planted to decorate a traffic island.

Harry and I, the two remaining, headed home on foot. On our way we had to pass the local bus station and I had some difficulty in persuading Harry that borrowing an unattended double decker bus would probably be more trouble than it was worth. I seem to remember telling him that there wouldn't be enough fuel in the tank because they drained all the diesel every night in order to stop people stealing the buses. I remember wondering why they didn't just lock them up but consoling myself with the knowledge that life is always full of mysteries.

Thwarted in his yearning to drive a double decker bus home my chum insisted on our borrowing a half full grit bin instead, insisting that those students with cars would think it a kindly gesture. We somehow managed to drag the bin all the way home with us, leaving it inconveniently situated in the entrance to the small car park outside the Hall of Residence. A week later it took a lorry, a crane and eight highways employees to return it to its ordained location. (Three months later Harry did successfully borrow a double decker bus in order to get home without having to walk five miles.)

When we got back to our hall of residence we found that our companion, who had succeeded in walking home without acquiring a grit bin, was busily engaged in travelling about the 16 storey high building ripping plugs out of wash basins and baths. He had somehow acquired the idea that these were dangerous items if left in situ.

I was the only one of the trio still on speaking terms with sobriety and so I spent the rest of the evening making sure that neither of my hard working companions inhaled their vomit.

'It was the green chartreuse,' said Harry, staring at the contents of his stomach which were now no longer in his stomach and which bore a striking but startlingly inappropriate resemblance to diced carrots. 'I know I shouldn't have had the green chartreuse. It doesn't agree with me.'

I carefully lay my companions on their sides, in the position then officially approved for inebriated medical students (the rules governing first aid change with the seasons and modern recommended techniques seem designed more to confuse or offer variations for the sake of it than to save lives), placed waste paper baskets by their bedsides and covered them with fire blankets to keep them warm. Well, it seemed a good idea at the time.

The next day I went up to Scotland for a holiday with Dick. We were due to stay in a cottage owned by a benevolent uncle of his but when we arrived, after a two day journey in a vehicle which would have failed every aspect of an MOT test, we found that the uncle had mistakenly also let the cottage to a middle aged couple who had a pair of teenage daughters. Since we were by then a long way from any other potential accommodation, we all decided to share the cottage. We had one room downstairs and the family took the two bedrooms and dining room. The parents spent the week successfully hiding the two teenage daughters. The father was a fisherman who boasted, every day, of the fish he'd caught. On our final day we spotted him buying fish from a local fishmonger. He didn't see us and that evening boasted of yet another wonderful day's catch.

Later in the summer I went on a camping holiday in Italy with Harry. We shared a one man tent and learned to wear our shoes and thick socks at night to prevent our feet, which stuck out of the tent, being investigated too thoroughly by stray dogs in search of morsels of food.

It was my last summer of freedom and it seemed to last five minutes and forever.

At the beginning of the next term we found and shared a huge, rambling flat in a huge, Victorian building in Richmond Hill Road. (I believe the building still exists but has been turned into very elegant and expensive flats). And the world changed in oh so many ways. We were no longer first year students. We had survived the first year of the course. We had furniture and our own kitchen. I bought a 0.177 air rifle and we shot yoghurt cartons which we hung from a tree in the garden. The next door neighbour, a professional opera singer whose daily scales and vocal exercises were impressive rather than entertaining, complained to the police but the local constabulary liked us more than they liked her (we were always available to loan them traffic signs and other road furniture which had found its way into our flat and we let them take pot shots at the yoghurt cartons) so nothing came of her complaints. Very few pellets went into her garden, she never used the greenhouse and no one was seriously injured. We did offer to pay for the glass but our offer was ignored. She had a very noisy dog, I remember. One of those small ones used as a fashion accessory. It yapped all day long.

Tom, Dick, Harry and I learned many new, pointless and anti-social skills. We learned for example, to remove the hinges from doors within a block of flats so that we could exchange the doors. This meant, inevitably, that keys did not fit locks and moody, difficult hospital registrars found themselves locked out of their accommodation. (The brighter ones learned that it was quicker to exchange keys than to try to put the doors back where they'd started.)

Tom, the pal who was treasurer of the bar subsequently became a very eminent surgeon and a member of the medical establishment. Dick became a radiologist and a pillar of his community. Harry, the fellow who wanted to borrow a double decker bus had a career as an anaesthetist and important committee member. None of them seemed to have suffered lasting damage from our evening. In those days it was called 'letting off steam' and it was an essential part of the process of turning callow youths into doctors. I suspect this inability to let off steam is at least partly responsible for the poor quality of young doctors these days.

And me?

Well, you know what happened to me.

I'm the only one who can talk about these things publicly without being ruined.

And I leave you, therefore, with one final thought.

If everything I have described had happened this year or last year it would have doubtless appeared in inglorious technicolour detail on social media and four medical careers would have ended before they had started.

There is a moral there, and it's not very well hidden.

Another Scary Story (My Bravest Moment)

After I'd been working as a GP for a few months I was telephoned by a doctor working in another local practice and asked if I would sign Part II of a cremation certificate.

I doubt if things have changed much but, back in the 1970s, when a patient died a doctor was required to sign a death certificate. He could only do this if he had seen the patient within two weeks and was happy to confirm a cause of death. You couldn't just write 'died' on the certificate and then sign it. There had to be a reason. One of my older partners, a conscientious GP called John Morris, told me that he used to visit very frail patients once a fortnight so that he could, if necessary, always be in a position to sign a certificate without the relatives being upset by there being a post mortem. I tried to do the same.

There was no fee for signing a death certificate but if a deceased patient was due to be cremated, two special cremation forms had to be signed – to make sure that a patient who'd been murdered wasn't being quickly cremated to remove the evidence. (This wasn't much help when the doctor was the murderer as, for example, was the case with the serial killer Dr Harold Shipman. The infamous Shipman succeeded in murdering around 250 of his patients and got away with it for years before the authorities did anything about the extraordinary mortality rate among his patients.)

One of the cremation forms was usually signed by the doctor who had signed the death certificate and the second would be signed by a colleague from another practice. There were fees for signing these two forms and although these would, in the end, be passed on to the relatives responsible for the funeral, the fees were usually paid directly by the funeral director. And the fees, around £25 at the time I seem to remember, were always paid in cash.

(For junior hospital doctors paid, in those days, a pittance of around £650 a year, from which board and lodging was deducted, the fee for signing a cremation certificate was the price of a very good night out. This notable windfall was always referred to as 'ash cash' and I apologise for this irreverence.)

Because the signing fee was always handed over in cash by the supervising undertaker (usually in a discreet envelope so that the pretence of professional dignity could be maintained) there were alleged to be some doctors who regarded 'ash cash' as a non-taxable perk. I remember that when a local doctor was getting divorced, his wife's lawyer threatened to expose this small fraud if his client didn't get the settlement she demanded. I'm told that the other partners lived in terror for several weeks.

Most GPs seemed to have a 'cremation form partner' in another practice and the two doctors would always telephone each other when Part Two forms needed to be signed. I never managed to arrange anything quite so convenient and profitable and used simply to telephone nearby practices at random until I found a doctor happy to comply. It was never difficult to speak to a doctor under those circumstances. I found that if I told a receptionist that I wondered if Dr X would be available to sign a Part Two cremation certificate the more venal practitioners would be on the phone within seconds. With some doctors, I doubt if any emergency was ever answered as speedily as a request to sign a Part Two certificate. Kerching! Another £25 in the back pocket.

Despite my failure to acquire a 'partner' (probably because most of the local doctors were already spoken for in this regard) I was occasionally called upon to pop along to a local undertaker, certify that Mr or Mrs Suchandsuch was truly dead, with no obvious signs of foul play, sign the required certificate, collect my fee and totter back home with a slim but welcome envelope tucked safely in my inside jacket pocket.

I can still remember the first time I had to sign the second half of a cremation certificate. I hadn't been a GP for more than a few months.

In hospitals, of course, most dead bodies are storied in the mortuary, hidden somewhere out of sight but all well organised. Local undertakers usually had their own mortuaries too. But, as luck would have it, the undertaker looking after the corpse I had been asked to certify had stored half a dozen of his customers in a nearby garage. I have no idea why this was. Maybe his mortuary was full, maybe they were having the place decorated, or maybe they had rented it out for a party.

Whatever the reason might have been, I was given the key, told that all the cadavers had their names on toe tags and asked to let myself in, do the necessary and then lock up before returning the key to the undertaker and collecting my envelope.

I'm sure that there must have been a light in the garage, and equally sure that there would have also been an appropriate light switch somewhere. But I couldn't find the switch and so couldn't turn on the light. And with the door closed I couldn't see a thing. I didn't like to leave the door open in case passers-by were shocked by the sight of half a dozen dead bodies lying on tables and trolleys in what seemed from the outside to be a pretty normal garage – though far larger than a usual garage and obviously designed to take three cars.

I pulled out my tiny pen torch (more usually used for peering down throats) and waved it around. It was, inevitably, woefully inadequate. It was intended for closer, more specific work such as investigating a pair of tonsils, than for illuminating a large garage. The walls were decorated with rows of tools and old tyres, and cans of what smelt like petrol were stored around the edges.

Eventually, however, I found the toe tag I was looking for.

I put the non-functional end of the torch between my teeth, shone the light on the shrouded cadaver and pulled back the covering sheet so that I could commence my examination. No one had ever told me what to do when certifying that a patient had died but I always thought that listening to the chest and trying for a pulse was a good starting point. After doing this I went on to test a few reflexes with my patella hammer.

It was pitch-black, I was alone in a garage with an unidentified number of corpses and I nearly jumped out of my skin when a hand brushed against the front of my thigh.

Moving my head and the torch, I managed to discover that the hand belonged to the cadaver I was about to examine. The arm and hand had slipped off the rather narrow table on which it had been placed and was now dangling free. I assumed that the undertaker had run short of gurneys and trolleys and was using old kitchen furniture for storing the customers.

With my heart beating fast enough for both of us, I gently lifted up the arm and laid it back on the table.

I then turned my attention back to the patient's chest.

And was again frightened out of my wits as the deceased patient exhaled loudly, clearly and convincingly.

Dead bodies do that, of course. Air in the lungs can escape if a body is moved a little.

At that point I decided that I needed a little fresh air and some reassuring daylight. I lunged clumsily for where I thought the door was situated. As I did so I knocked against another body, this time lying on a wheeled gurney. And this time both half a leg and the whole of an arm fell off the gurney and banged into my side.

I lunged for the place where I thought the door should be, found the handle and flung the door open, nearly knocking over a young woman pushing a pram. She, seeing a wide eyed man holding a torch in his mouth and emerging from a darkened room in which dead bodies could be glimpsed, didn't hang round for explanations. Pushing the pram, she ran off down the street as quickly as she could. If there is ever an Olympic event which involves pushing a fully laden pram for half a mile they should find that woman and put her in the team. She will be older now but I'm confident that given the right incentive (such as a glimpse of a man with a torch in his mouth coming out of a garage full of dead bodies) she'll still be capable of a decent turn of speed.

My attempted reassurances were delivered to the back of a woman who wasn't going to slow down for anyone or anything. She's probably still running and who can blame her.

I shut the door behind me, looked up at the sky, took some deep breaths and waited for a minute or two for my heart rate to get back below 200.

And then came the brave bit: I went back into the garage, armed only with a penlight, a stethoscope and a plastic reflex hammer.

It didn't take long to confirm that the body I'd been hired to examine was properly dead. And I then checked the body which had half fallen off the gurney. That too wasn't going anywhere. I locked up, returned the key, collected my envelope and went home. The shaking didn't last more than an hour or so.

For no good reason that I'm aware of, it was months before I was asked to sign another Part Two cremation certificate.

And, to be honest, I didn't mind the wait one little bit.

A Kindness

My wife, Antoinette, has a gift for doing unexpected, small kindnesses for strangers.

I was parked outside a local pharmacy one day, waiting for her to come out with her prescription medicines, when I saw her appear with the requisite little paper bag clutched in one hand (I am always pleased to see her with this in her hand since the pharmacy sometimes takes weeks to obtain her essential medication). I couldn't help noticing that she was followed, close behind, by an elderly couple.

When Antoinette reached the car, the male half of the couple reached out, tapped her on the arm and said something. I couldn't hear what. He seemed very happy. He and his wife then insisted on shaking Antoinette by the hand.

'What was that about?' I asked, when she got into the car.

'They were looking at hot water bottles,' replied Antoinette. 'But they didn't have enough money to buy a hot water bottle each so they wouldn't buy just the one.'

'So you bought them the other bottle?'

Antoinette blushed a little. 'Well, no, I bought both hot water bottles and gave them to the old couple.'

In a charity shop she bought an old man a thick blanket he had been fondling covetously for five minutes. In Paris she gave all the money in her purse to a woman whom she spotted hunting around in rubbish bins for food. She is always fair game for beggars and scroungers.

This morning, we were sitting in the conservatory watching a seagull standing underneath the bird feeders waiting for small birds to come and spill seed for it to eat. The bullfinch sprinkles ten times as much as he eats, constantly searching for just the right sunflower heart. Be he wasn't there and there wasn't much seed being spilt. It had been raining for half an hour and suddenly the shower turned into an unexpected thunderstorm. The seagull remained where he was; defiant and determined. The small birds had more sense and stayed sheltering in the bushes.

Suddenly, Antoinette picked up a packet of sunflower hearts, grabbed a hat and rushed out into the storm. When she reached the feeders, which are about thirty yards from the house, she threw some sunflower hearts on the ground and then hurried back to the conservatory.

She was soaked.

We sat together and watched as the happy seagull gobbled up the unexpected treats.

CB Fry

C.B. Fry was without a doubt the greatest sportsman the world has ever seen. Fry played cricket and football for England and played in an FA Cup Final. He played rugby for Oxford University and held the world long jump record.

In addition to his athletic achievements, he was a Captain in the Navy and wrote a number of books. He worked as one of the first radio commentators and was a regular panellist on radio programmes such as Any Questions and the Brains Trust. He did tons of other stuff too. If I try to list his achievements I'll be depressed for a week. In his seventies he was still fit enough to be able to jump backwards, from a standing position, onto a mantelpiece. The Albanian people were so impressed by the numerous activities, skills and talents of this English superman that they asked him to be their King. They probably fancied a monarch who could jump backwards onto a mantelpiece. It would put him head and shoulders above monarchs who simply waved and simpered. Fry declined, presumably because he couldn't fit it into his schedule.

Oh, and he also edited a magazine.

The eponymous magazine which Fry edited was stuffed with amazing stories.

So for example, the edition for October 1904 contained an extraordinary article about Aston Villa Football Club, at the time one of the most successful football clubs in the country. On one Scottish tour the gate for the match against Dumbarton was just £5.00. The local officials were too ashamed to divide the proceeds (as had been the arrangement) and so gave Aston Villa the whole £5.00 and entertained them to tea.

The magazine contained an article by H.Hesketh Prichard (the author of an extraordinary travel book about Patagonia, a county cricketer, a novelist and the man who invented sniping) about a hunting trip in Newfoundland. Prichard, like Fry, is a man whose achievements are too much for ordinary mortals to comprehend.

And there was an item about Fry himself who is pictured driving a beautiful Clement-Talbot motor car. Fry reported that he used to drive himself about the country to attend cricket matches in which he was playing. The article describes how, having spent the day fielding in a match against Sussex at Hove, the intrepid Fry set off to drive to Derby with just a planned stop in London for 'refreshment'. 'I have been looking forward to that motor ride all day,' said Fry of his planned 191 mile trip.

(It was perhaps just as well that the 10mph limit imposed in 1861 had been lifted. Prior to that the limit had been 2 mph in towns and 4 mph in rural areas. The raising of the limit to 14 mph in 1896 is remembered by the annual London to Brighton Veteran Car Run. In 1903, the limit had been raised to 20 mph but no one took much notice of the limit since speedometers were as rare among police officers as among motorists. It is safe to assume that Mr Fry didn't worry too much about speed limits. Besides, no policeman would have dared stop C.B.Fry.)

And there was an article explaining how to save money by buying a motor car in Paris and importing it to England. It was reported that a car costing £750 in London could be purchased for £450 in Paris.

If you see a copy of *C.B.Fry's Magazine of Action and Outdoor Life* for sale I recommend you snap it up. There isn't a magazine published today that is half as much fun.

An English Gentleman

When I was a GP, one of my partners was a genuine English gentleman.

We used to watch cricket together at Edgbaston, Worcester and Taunton cricket grounds.

Once, at Edgbaston, he arrived with a companion I'd never met before.

My partner was subdued during the morning's play and since I knew that his wife had left him for another man, and was divorcing him, I naturally assumed that this was the reason.

At lunchtime, the stranger departed temporarily and I asked my partner how he knew his companion.

'He's the man my wife has run off with,' replied my partner.

I stared at him, disbelievingly.

'I'd only met him once,' said my partner. 'It was before I knew about him and my wife. He asked if I'd take him to a cricket match one day.'

'And you said yes, obviously.'

'I did.'

'But why have you brought him now that you know…?'

'Because I'd said I would,' replied my partner softly.

And that, I think, is as good a definition of a gentleman as you'll find.

As for the other fellow…well, I can't say I'll ever think of him as much of a gentleman.

Columns Galore

I never did much journalism. I wrote some features and did a few interviews when I was young but I quickly found that I wasn't much good at asking strangers nosy questions. I realise this may sound absurd, since I spent ten years of my life working as a doctor and asking strangers nosy questions but it's true.

Doctors have to ask patients the most intrusive questions – questions which would be regarded as impertinent if not downright rude if asked in any other circumstances.

'How often do you open your bowels?' 'What colour is the discharge?' 'Have you had sex with anyone other than your husband?' 'At what point in the discussion with your husband did you feel that you were losing the argument and that it was time to introduce the carving knife into the conversation?'

That sort of stuff.

(I should point out that it was my experience that patients were often just as ready to tear down the normal barriers to conversation when talking to their doctor. I once saw a couple who complained that their sex life was entirely unsatisfactory. It was the wife who initiated the complaint. She reported that her husband could only manage between 70 and 90 what she called 'ins and outs' before ejaculating. It transpired that the wife, dissatisfied with her husband's performance, had taken to counting the number of times her husband moved inside her before concluding the entertainment in the traditional way. It was, I suppose, sex by numbers. My initial contribution to this discussion was to ask the woman if she counted to herself or out loud. She reported that she counted out loud. My feeling, expressed rather timidly, was that it seemed possible that this might not have added to the quality of the experience for either partner. This suspicion was enthusiastically supported by the husband. For a while during this conversation I feared that I was a victim of some strange candid camera type of encounter. I did tell this bizarre story in a very early book of mine and I sometimes wonder if any reader was ever inspired to follow the unhappy wife's example and count her husband's efforts. One thing I did discover during my years in general practice is that the world is a far stranger place than most people imagine. I used to see the couple once a week for a while. They kept details of the 'ins and outs' in a small black notebook. I made various suggestions, which may or may not have helped. In the end they just stopped coming. Or, perhaps, 'attending' might be a more appropriate word. I rather doubt if things ended happily.)

Getting back to where I was before that small aside, I can only explain that my natural shyness and reticence were temporarily suppressed when I was a doctor since I was, as it were, acting in officio. I never wore a white coat but I had a desk (which I always kept to one side so that it wasn't a barrier), some small authority and a badge of office (a stethoscope).

Why couldn't my subconscious use the same trick if I were acting as a journalist? Your guess is as good as mine. I interviewed many people for television programmes and I was painfully bad at it and gave it up quite early – though perhaps not as early as I should have done.

I never had the killer instinct to be a journalist.

Real journalists will do anything to get a story they want. They will (sometimes literally) step on anyone who stands in their way.

I remember a chum telling me a story about a father and son who both worked for national newspapers – both of them for tabloid newspapers.

The two of them were at home having dinner together one evening when the telephone rang. The wife of one and the mother of the other answered the telephone and passed on a message to the two men at the table.

I can't remember what the story was, and it doesn't really matter. The only thing that matters is that whatever had happened, was happening or was about to happen was local and they both instantly knew that they could get there before anyone else.

Old-time journalists would do anything and everything to get the story first. Even if their paper wasn't going to be put to bed for several hours they still wanted to be the first to phone the story into their news editor.

The two men had their cars parked outside the house. They were parked side by side so that if one of them wanted to make a quick getaway he could do so without waiting for the other. The son, being younger and nimbler got out of the house first. He had slip-on shoes, which didn't involve the tying of laces, and he didn't bother with a jacket. The father had to tie his shoelaces and struggle into a coat.

By the time the father got out of the house, the son's car was just a noise in the distance. The father got into his car, started the engine and knew before he had reversed off the driveway that he had a flat tyre. When he got out of the car he discovered that he had two flat tyres. And they hadn't gone flat because of a faulty valve or some other natural disaster. Both tyres had been stabbed with what later turned out to have been the son's penknife.

That's how journalists used to behave.

I worked for newspapers for most of my life but I was never a journalist.

I started by writing features which required nothing much more than an imagination. When I did need an input from outside sources, I usually found ways to obtain the information I required without actually having to speak to people.

For example, for one English Cup Final I wrote a feature for a national newspaper assessing the psychological strengths of the 22 footballers involved. The idea was to predict the outcome by looking at how well the players would cope with the stress of the occasion. For the purposes of this feature I prepared a questionnaire which the paper's chief football correspondent handed to the managers at the two clubs involved. The two clubs then handed the questionnaires to all their players, including the reserves, and the paper I was working for at the time (*The Daily Star*) sent the questionnaires to me by post. I then wrote the feature which took up two pages of the paper's pre-match feature. I didn't have to speak to anyone which suited me fine.

(Afterwards, I was about to throw away the two dozen or so questionnaires, all of which had been filled in by hand, and signed by the players, when I discovered, by chance, that the woman who served in my local newsagents was married to a man who was a devoted follower of one of the clubs. I earned myself a good many brownie points by giving her the bundle of questionnaires to hand to her husband.)

Mainly, I was a columnist.

Over the years I wrote columns for scores of different newspapers all around the world

I started early in this rather specialised trade. While I was at medical school I wrote a weekly column for the university newspaper, a weekly column for a medical newspaper called *Medical News*, an anonymous weekly column for a paper called *Hospital Times* (for which I pretended to be a young hospital doctor) a weekly syndicated medical column (for which I claimed to be a GP) and a variety of columns for small, usually monthly, magazines. If writing columns is a disease then I had it in spades.

Later, I wrote five national newspaper columns in the UK (under three different names). Four of the columns were for tabloids and one was for a broadsheet. I wrote columns for daily newspapers, Sunday newspapers, general magazines, magazines for women, magazines for girls, magazines for doctors and a magazine for cricket lovers. I wrote special columns for the *Sunday Scot*, the *Glasgow Evening Times* and the *Sunday Independent* in the West Country. Most of the columns were syndicated around the world, which I especially liked because when I received a syndication cheque from a newspaper or magazine in Australia, South Africa or India it seemed like money for doing nothing.

I resigned from nearly all of the columns, usually over trivial issues, except the *Sunday Correspondent* which, sadly, disappeared of its own accord. Most of the resignations I regretted.

For decades I wrote two competing syndicated columns (one under my name and one not) which were printed in scores of large evening papers in the UK and in papers and magazines around the world. I wrote a column which went to weekly local papers too. And I wrote the agony column for what was then one of the big Sunday newspapers. I'm afraid I have to confess that all the questions and answers were made up because I never liked the idea of passing judgement on people's lives. Besides, the letters I received were always far too complex for a slick answer in 25 to 100 words. Occasionally, people would complain in the media about the advice I'd given them. But they were always lying because I never gave advice to real people. I used to write the answers first because I found that once I'd written the answers it was easy to create the questions. I wasn't the only agony aunt to do this. I wrote an agony column for a girls' magazine called *Over 21* too. (The magazine's title was misleading. The readers were generally under 21.) And I was the original agony aunt on BBC television.

I quickly discovered that the secret of writing a column is to build a personal relationship with the reader. It's the same thing that successful radio presenters manage to do. They always share some of themselves with their listeners. Television, in contrast, is a far more superficial medium which simply requires its performers to have beautiful looks and beautiful hair. There was never any room outside France for someone looking as thoroughly debauched as Serge Gainsbourg.

The last four decades of the 20th century were glorious years in Fleet Street. Journalists on the national newspapers were not just given huge expense accounts (one features editor on the *Sunday Mirror* used to welcome my visits by popping to the accountant's office and picking up a thick wad of £10 notes, known in the office as 'brown drinking vouchers' as expenses money) but they were actually supplied with virtually unlimited amounts of alcohol 'in house'. Editors on some papers, even editors who were quite low down on the feeding chain, were given several bottles of alcohol every week by a man who brought the stuff round on a large trolley. Editors in the features departments would be allowed a dozen bottles of wine a week to keep in their desk cupboard. It was quite common for journalists to be drunk after lunch. Most were never drunk but never quite sober; always just this side of tipsy, and probably never sober enough to drive a motor car or operate an electric pencil sharpener.

Newspapers were wildly overstaffed in those days, with vast numbers of editors employed, and there were journalists on the staff of the nationals who hadn't had anything they had written published for many months. Overstaffing wasn't confined to the print unions. Some of the staff were so underemployed that they spent most of their time writing articles for outside magazines or popping out to Bush House to record something for one of the BBC's foreign stations.

Money flowed like water in the papers in those days. These days journalists and feature writers are paid a fraction of the sort of fees which used to be paid thirty or forty years ago. I would take a few ideas to London and sit with an editor for a quarter of an hour while I outlined the features I had in mind.

'What do you want for that one?'

'Five grand?'

'Done.'
'What do want for that one?'
'It'll make a spread. Ten grand?'
'Done.'

I mention these figures not as a boast but as an illustration of a time gone by; a time when ten grand was ten grand and a not indecent annual salary. At my age, I see no point in being coy. On the other hand, for small circulation magazines I wrote columns without charging a fee at all.

I'd write one or two of the features on the train home later that day. The rest I'd write while watching cricket at Edgbaston or Worcester cricket ground.

Several times a paper would take out television advertising for a feature which I hadn't even written and which existed only as an idea in my head.

Those were wonderful and rather silly days.

It is difficult to believe that national newspapers could have ever made a profit, particularly since editors' desk drawers were full of manuscripts which had been bought and which had never been used (and never would be). I was lucky in that most of my articles were published but I always arranged to be paid 'on delivery' and never 'on publication'.

What happened in many cases was that a feature editor would commission an article, or buy one which had been submitted speculatively, and then show it to the editor (the editor of the paper) who would be enthusiastic. Then something would come up. Serial rights to a popular new book would be available. A celebrity's agent would offer a kiss and tell story. And the commissioned article would be put aside.

One of the oddities of national newspaper journalism in those days was that if an article wasn't published within a day or two of being purchased it would probably never be published. The enthusiasm faded. Facts would have to be re-checked (and the tabloid newspapers, which were the ones I did most work for, were far more assiduous about checking facts than the broadsheets which would pretty well print anything without checking it) and something which had been appeared timely and relevant the day it was bought would probably appear old hat a week later.

The pubs in and around Fleet Street must have done very well out of journalists in those days. Most would meet at eateries such as Joe Allen's (a short walk from Fleet Street for the healthy and a cab ride for most) and auction off the receipt at the end of a meal. There might be a dozen journalists having a meal together. No one would go through the bill to see who had eaten or drunk what, but instead various journalists would bid for the right to pay the bill. This was a business transaction, not an act of philanthropy.

If the bill came to £500, for example, the winning bid for the right to pay it would probably be £50 or £100 or sometimes even more. The winner would use his personal credit card to pay the £500 bill for everyone's meal and take the receipt back to his office where the paper's accountant would pay him back the total on the receipt in cash. His profit would be the size of the bill minus whatever he had paid over for the right to pay the bill, plus the tax relief on the size of the bill on his personal credit card. The £50 or £100 he had paid would be shared among the rest of the journalists at the table. So they'd have a free meal with a cash bonus. And it wasn't entirely unknown for waiters to give empty receipt forms to journalists – in return for an overlarge tip. (All the people involved in what was, without a doubt, an outrageous and illegal scam, are now no longer with us so there is no point in anyone asking me for any names.)

One well-known journalist nearly always won the auction. He carried a small pocket calculator and quickly and surreptitiously worked out what he could afford to pay and still make a profit on the deal. He was the only person I ever knew who always had a stout rubber band around his wallet. I suspect that said a good deal about his attitude to money. He was one of three Fleet Street journalists I knew who drove Rolls Royce motor cars.

In those days newspapers often bought serial rights to books and that was good fun and profitable too. Magazines such as *People's Friend* and *My Weekly*, magazines with huge circulations at the time, used to buy my novels, cut them up and run them as seemingly never ending serials. Weekly instalments from a book of 100,000 words would run every week for six months. And the Sunday tabloids were always looking for books to serialise.

The *Sunday Mirror* bought serial rights to my book *Bodypower* and seemed to run extracts for ever. There's a section in the book describing a scientific experiment in which women had succeeded in enlarging the size of their breasts with self-hypnosis. The features editor hired a group of young models, I instructed them and we had their breasts measured and then re-measured a week or two later. The measuring was all done by an independent nurse. It was a high risk strategy because if the girls' breasts hadn't got larger I'd have looked a fool. But things went incredibly well and the breasts all grew notably to everyone's delight. There was, I seem to remember, a double page spread photo of me standing alongside a row of very happy looking models and holding a very large mock-up of a ruler that someone in the art department had made. The extracts went round the world and did the sales of the (quite serious) book no harm at all. It was my first book of mine that entered all the major bestseller lists.

I have never seen a group of newspaper executives as excited as the editors of the *Sunday Mirror* were on the Saturday afternoon before the news of our 'experiment' was published. Other editors and journalists watched in astonishment (and some concern) as *Sunday Mirror* staff celebrated. The paper's circulation duly rose noticeably. There were TV advertisements, special T-shirts promoting *Bodypower* and huge posters stuck up all over the country.

Robert Wilson, the chain-smoking, gin-loving features editor of the *Sunday Mirror* at the time of *Bodypower*, became a good friend and used to visit me at my home in the country. The first time he came to visit he confessed that he'd bought 200 cigarettes and three bottles of gin before he boarded the train because he didn't know how long the train journey was going to be. I pointed out that it was only a two and a half hour journey. He responded by explaining that trains sometimes broke down, stranding passengers in the middle of the countryside. He's gone now, bless his golden memory, but he was a kind and gentle fellow who had written three science fiction novels and talked knowledgeably about Nietzsche. I miss his smile, ever-twinkling eyes and quiet voice.

An Editor

I have been an editor only three times in my life and on two of those occasions I was also the publisher.

The exception was when I was appointed editor of a new and, it has to be said, fairly short lived medical publication called the *British Clinical Journal*. The *BCJ* (as it was known to its friends and quite possibly to its enemies too) was intended to provide doctors with sharp, incisive articles designed to entertain while informing and, also, to make them think.

In my early years as a medical student I had contributed to many medical journals, magazines and newspapers (including the *British Medical Journal, The Lancet, Nursing Times* some esoteric publications such as the *Journal of Medical Ethics* and around a dozen other publications) and I may be wrong but I don't remember entertaining, informing or making the reader think being high on the list of intentions among most of the editors. Most medical publications were, it seemed to me, simply looking for material to separate the endless pages of drug company advertising. I always felt this was as true of the medical journals with big reputations as of all the others.

The *British Clinical Journal* had a subscription price but I don't think many people actually paid money to receive a copy. Most of the copies were, like everything else, simply posted out to every doctor whose name was on the medical register.

I cannot remember how I came to be hired to be the editor but I rather think I replied to one of the small, classified adverts in the back of one of the medical journals – probably the *British Medical Journal*, which always ran a variety of intriguing ads from ships looking for doctors and private practitioners in Harley Street looking for assistants to do the work while they played golf or counted their money.

The *BCJ* had offices in Wardour Street and I worked there a day and a half a week, staying overnight at the National Liberal Club in Whitehall Place which was, in those days, a wonderful, old-fashioned London club which had not yet become home to a tribe of woke liberals. I had a bedroom on the third floor and tea was delivered every morning by a dear old lady who struggled so much with the weight of a cup of tea that the cup rattled constantly in the saucer. If you asked her she'd open the curtains, as per Jeeves, so that you could see what the weather was like. The only bathroom was cavernous and freezing cold except in rare heat-waves. At breakfast there was a choice of a solitary table for one or a place at a long, communal table. Hot food was served in cloches, those silver plated dishes with lids, cornflakes and so on were served in individual packets and the bread basket included individual Hovis loaves. The coffee was very black, very thick and entirely undrinkable. I spilt some on my trousers once and had to throw them away when a huge hole appeared just above the knee.

I was working part time as a GP at the same time as I was editing the *British Clinical Journal* and so I rode up and down every week on the intercity train between Paddington and Coventry. In those distant days trains served good food in first class and you could dine there with a second class ticket. I ate many meals on British Rail trains and it was always an experience. Breakfast, I remember, was always a particularly fine event. I could easily stretch out a meal for the best part of two hours, never needing to go back to my seat in the second class carriage. This was a jolly wheeze because the cost of a meal and a second class ticket was, I remember, considerably less than the cost of a first class ticket.

Making me an editor was a mistake, of course. I should have never applied for the job, they should have never offered me the job and I should never have taken it. The key to success with a free magazine of any type, but particularly one for doctors, is to keep the advertisers happy. They, after all, are the publication's only source of income. The editorial, settled down in between the adverts, needs to be anodyne. Since our magazine was being delivered to doctors the main advertisers were, of course, drug companies. (The one exception was a regular ad for an airline. This puzzled me for a while until I discovered that the publisher gave the airline free advertising and they gave him free airline tickets.)

Right from the start, under my direction, the *BCJ* could not have worked harder at annoying drug companies. I already had a reputation for attacking the pharmaceutical industry since I had written a number of articles for the national press questioning drug industry morality.

And, surprise, surprise, the main article in one of our first issues in 1971 dealt with psychotropic drugs (especially benzodiazepines such as Valium). We had organised a symposium where a number of speakers made clear their fears about these drugs and it was a terrific issue, well ahead of the rest of the medical literature, the medical establishment, the medical profession as a whole. It was ahead of the press, TV and the radio too. I was quite proud of it. We had a wonderful, bright cover too – with a man's head made up entirely of brightly coloured capsules and pills which I assume I must have provided.

We (for which read I) did some promotion for the issue and I had a bag full of little bottles which contained different benzodiazepines which I would take with me to television studios. At one studio in Birmingham I was waiting for an interview to start, and was sitting looking at the bottles which I had given to the studio manager for the props man to lay out on a low, coffee style table in front of me, when I leant forwards and moved a couple of the bottles around so that I could see the labels more clearly.

Suddenly, there was a yell. The lights went out and men in soft shoes started rushing around shouting at one another. I didn't have the foggiest idea what was happening but was wrongly content that it had nothing to do with me.

'I'm afraid we've got a problem with the union,' said the man who was due to interview me. He'd rushed into the studio from the make-up department and still had a little white cloth around his neck to protect his shirt collar.

I looked at him and like to think I raised an eyebrow quizzically but I probably just asked him why. (If anyone ever films this book I think I'd like the actor playing me to raise an eyebrow quizzically.)

'Did you move some of the bottles?' asked the interviewer.

I confessed that I had.

'You can't do that.'

'But they're my bottles of pills.'

'Yes, but the props guys laid them out and you touched them. They're the only people allowed to move things in the studio.' He looked very unhappy. 'They now say they won't work with you and if you stay there'll be a walk out.'

'Are any of the props men medically qualified?' I asked.

'Oh no, I'm sure they aren't,' he said.

'Then they can't touch these,' I said, pointing to the pills. 'They are all prescription only medicines.'

The interviewer stared at me for a moment and a small smile appeared. 'Just wait a moment, will you?' he asked. He then walked away and came back a moment or two later with a fellow in jeans and a sweatshirt.

'This is Geoff, our Union guy,' said the interview, introducing us. 'Would you tell him what you just told me?'

I explained that the bottles all contained prescription drug and that only a registered medical practitioner or a registered pharmacist could handle them.

'You mean, it's like a union thing?' said Geoff.

'Exactly,' I replied. 'I'm a member of the British Medical Association. It's my trade union.'

Geoff nodded and apologised to me. 'Only the doctor touches the pill bottles,' he shouted. 'If we need anything moved ask him and he'll do it.' The various members of the studio crew (there were always a good many people working in a television studio in those days) all nodded or murmured their understanding.

The interviewer was now struggling to suppress a grin.

When the interview was over and I left the studio, the director walked me to the exit where my taxi was waiting. Classy as ever, I had my pill bottles in a plastic supermarket bag. There were tears in the director's eyes. He clasped one of my hands with both of his. 'Oh thank you, thank you,' he murmured. 'That was one of the most wonderful moments in my life.'

Anyway, that is something of an aside. I need to get back to the story about the *British Clinical Journal*.

After we had published a few issues, the publisher and I, on our way back from having lunch with a group of GPs near Bournemouth (I have absolutely no idea why we'd gone there) called in at the offices of a drug company which the publisher was trying to persuade to advertise in the *British Clinical Journal*.

'What do I have to do to persuade you to advertise with us?' asked the publisher, trying to suppress a feeling of quiet desperation.

The drug company executive paused for a moment and then pointed a finger straight at me. 'Sack him,' he said.

He wasn't joking.

And so my tenure as a magazine editor came to an end a short while later. It was fun while it lasted.

Though I can't remember why we'd gone all that way, I do remember that after that meeting we drove to the station, dumped the hire car and caught a train back to London. I then travelled across London to Paddington Station where I caught a train to Coventry. I then picked up my car and drove back in time for my evening surgery. I think trains must have been more reliable in those days. I travelled about so much that I regularly used to climb aboard trains while they were moving. You could do that in those days.

For a long time, I used to catch an early morning train to London, take a taxi to the TV AM studios, talking about something or other, take a taxi back to Paddington, catch a train to Coventry and drive back in time for a morning surgery.

How was that possible? I have no idea.

I remember patients coming in, sitting down opposite me and staring for a moment before telling me that they'd just watched me on a television programme and how did I do that.

After my tenure at the *British Clinical Journal* finished (not long before the journal itself was nothing but a memory) I avoided taking on any editorial responsibility for a few years until I decided that the world was once again ready to allow me to sit in an editor's chair.

This time I decided to avoid all potential conflict with advertisers, shareholders and publishers by not having any advertisers, shareholders or publishers. I founded my own magazine.

Deciding that I wanted a title which sounded important and substantial, I called my new journal the *European Medical Journal*, since surprisingly perhaps there didn't seem to be one already. As publisher and owner I appointed myself editor-in-chief, editor and columnist.

The journal was intended to be a vehicle for doctors and scientists who wanted to air substantial, well researched alternative viewpoints. The one rule was that the *EMJ* would publish nothing which supported or relied on animal experimentation. I had long been an opponent of vivisection which I regarded (and still regard) as nothing more than a convenient way for the pharmaceutical industry to provide itself and the regulators with false evidence allowing them to pretend that the products they are selling are safe when they know damned well that they aren't.

To begin with I wrote much or most of the material for the *EMJ* myself (using a variety of names) but as time went by and subscriptions went up so I slowly made contact with doctors looking for an outlet for their original ideas. I also entered into working relationships with journals in Australia and America. The rising number of subscribers was not hindered by my giving certificates to new subscribers entitling them to regard themselves as Fellows of the European Medical Association. I had created the *European Medical Association* at the same time as I'd founded the *Journal* and had, remarkably, been able to patent both that name and the title *European Medical Journal*.

There was even a German edition of the *EMJ*, published as an insert in a big selling German magazine for fans of alternative medicine. I had met the editor and publisher of the German magazine at a conference in Landau in Switzerland where I'd spoken about animal experimentation.

When I started publishing books of my own which mainstream publishers considered too risky (usually for legal reasons – in other words they were worried that they would be sued) I used the imprint *European Medical Journal*. *Betrayal of Trust* was the first proper hardback medical book I published under the *EMJ* imprint and it did much better than I or anyone else had expected. There were several reprints and a paperback edition and we sold over 12,000 copies in hardback alone which was probably around 11,999 more than most people expected. I am still using the *EMJ* imprint today for books on medical matters. From time to time some idiot will protest that I have sold out to big euro-business because my books are published by an imprint which sounds as if it is part of the establishment. In reality, of course, nothing could be further from the truth.

Sadly, the *EMJ* itself came to a rather abrupt halt as a result of some litigation which involved the pharmaceutical industry, private detectives, a firm of solicitors who had more cuttings about me than I knew existed (and who also had copies of business letters which I had thought were as private as business letters can be and which were certainly not relevant to the lawsuit) and a writ server who had such a huge bundle of papers to hand me that he pushed them through the cat flap rather than the letterbox. Innocently, I had refused to open the door because I thought the writ server had to hand me the papers he was serving. Apparently, and rather disappointingly, poking them through the cat flap serves just as well.

A few years after the sad demise of the *EMJ*, I was back in the editor's chair with a newsletter called *Dr Vernon Coleman's Health Letter*. Once again I was the publisher and sole shareholder so arguments at board meetings were short lived. Antoinette and I wrote all the content between us.

(Actually, there was a fourth publication: a small specialist newsletter for benzodiazepine addicts. That was published in the 1980s and was distributed without any charge. The postage bills were painful. This was intended to be a source of medical information for people who were suspicious of the medical establishment, and much of the alternative medical establishment too, and who wanted a guide enabling them to assess and interpret medical information about benzodiazepine tranquillisers. The main purpose was to provide advice on how to stop taking the pills. I also included summaries of scientific papers which were relevant. And for a few years I edited and ran a fifth magazine devoted to the opposition of experiments on animals and to promoting an organisation called Plan 2000 which had founded.)

I was inspired to publish the health letter because I was a subscriber to a number of financial newsletters and I thought a medical letter, published once a month, would be useful. I never expected it to make money and in this, as in many of my endeavours, I was not disappointed, though if you don't count my time as being of any value (and muttered comments will be ignored) then the newsletter paid for itself. The circulation peaked at somewhere between 4,000 and 5,000 which was probably as good as could reasonably be expected. We had some very eminent subscribers. The Aga Khan, the Queen Mother and some well-known authors and doctors subscribed.

The problem, in retrospect was that I didn't charge enough. I set the annual subscription at £24.95 for twelve copies, and the cost of printing and posting quickly ate up most if not all of this – not leaving much to be spent on marketing and advertising. A friend of ours who lived in Paris wrote, edited and published a financial newsletter for which she charged $1,000 a year. A medical newsletter would have never sold at such a price but I should have charged more.

I was and am still very proud of *Dr Vernon Coleman's Health Letter*. My wife Antoinette, researched, wrote and edited many of the articles. However, eventually, the number of subscribers fell away, largely because the internet had become a massive source of free advice and opinion and partly because we couldn't keep on advertising to bring in new subscribers. Many of our readers were elderly and as they expired we struggled to replace them. Constantly rising postage and print prices constantly made things trickier.

And that was the end of my career as an editor.

There was, however, nearly a fourth. (Or is it a fifth, or a sixth? I'm losing count.)

For months, an old and dear friend called Tony worked with me on a magazine to be called *Dr Vernon Coleman's Health Secrets*. The magazine was designed as a colour magazine on glossy paper and Tony persuaded big retailers such as W.H.Smith to stock copies on their magazine shelves.

But the magazine was never printed or distributed and the proof copy I have shut away in a drawer is all that remains of it.

I wrote the whole of the first edition myself and it was one of the most exciting projects I had ever started. We hired a great art editor and the magazine looked fantastic.

In the end I killed the magazine and I still feel bad about it.

At the time I was writing four or five weekly columns, including two for national newspapers and one that was syndicated to around forty or fifty big regional and local papers and to papers in South Africa, India and Australia. I was also writing books and running my publishing business. And I was running a number of campaigns.

Tony was a great editor and the best of company and a very dear friend and I loved him dearly but when he sent me the final proof of the magazine, I was appalled. He had taken on the responsibility of editing the text, and the whole magazine was littered with literals and grammatical errors. I didn't have the time to go through and re-edit the magazine myself and I didn't have anyone at Publishing House with the time available to do it. The reason for the errors was simple: Tony was drinking heavily and he had become sloppy. I would have been a laughing stock if the magazine had appeared on the bookstalls with so many errors.

Like most journalists who had worked in Fleet Street, Tony had always been an enthusiastic drinker (and an enthusiastic and determined smoker too). When he first came to live in the country he asked in a local pub if anyone could help him with some carpentry work. A group of locals plied him with gin in an attempt to get him drunk enough to agree a high price for the work but in the end the locals drank themselves senseless trying to keep up with him. The carpenter among them signed a piece of paper agreeing to do the required work at a ridiculously low price.

I couldn't bring myself to tell Tony why I was killing the project and he took it harder than I'd expected. I think he knew it was his last hoorah and I think, secretly, he knew what the problem was. His wife took it even harder. She didn't invite me to the funeral when he died not long afterwards – inevitably, of a liver problem. I don't blame her.

Hindsight is a wonderful thing. I was wrong to kill the magazine. It was a stupid, stupid, stupid thing to do. I should have hired a professional proof-reader to line-edit each issue. But there wasn't time and I panicked. It cost me a friendship. I still miss Tony and it is the most painful of all my many professional regrets. Who knows whether the magazine would have been a success or a failure? That really doesn't matter a damn.

Every now and again I think about resurrecting the idea, though the time for it has passed. But it isn't because the time for it has gone that I don't do it.

It's because it was something I should have done with Tony.

At the Ritz

From time to time newspaper editors and publishers would invite me to have lunch with them. Publishers (or, more usually, editors employed by them) would usually take me to a small, modest eating establishment. Newspaper editors always preferred somewhere more fashionable and expensive where they could be seen and could wave to other editors or, ideally, to celebrities.

In my experience most ambitious celebrities (and that is most of them) would walk barefoot through a snake pit to do the kissy-kissy thing with a tabloid newspaper editor. In my experience, these luncheon meetings always seemed fraught with danger.

I once spent two hours waiting in the Savoy Hotel River Room Restaurant for an editor who was due to take me to lunch. On my way out of the hotel I saw him sitting, alone, in the Savoy Grill, waiting for me to turn up. We ended up having a very late lunch.

On another occasion the head waiter at the Savoy decided that the jacket I was wearing didn't fit the hotel's sartorial requirements. I ignored him and thereafter he returned the compliment.

One newspaper editor I worked for took me to lunch at the London Ritz hotel on Piccadilly. We were in the middle of what are, I think, known as contract negotiations. What this means is that we were going to discuss the amount of money he was going to pay me to write a column. As we walked into the hotel he pointed thing out to me and told me a little about the hotel's history and social significance. He nodded to the hall porter who, busy with a client, ignored him.

The editor concerned (whom I will call Adolf because that isn't his name, though it was the name by which he was known among his staff) can most accurately be described as pompous, aggressive and very self-important. He always liked to be recognised and greeted as though he were a combination of an African potentate and a rock star. He was a large man only in size. He must have weighed something in excess of 30 stones and was well over six feet tall. I think he had styled himself on Robert Maxwell, who always looked as if he were swimming around inside an ill-fitting fat suit. (Surely no one could really be that fat, was my thought when I shared a lift with Maxwell. It was a lift for eight but the two of us filled it. Never mind, I thought, I once shared a lift for two people with a Liberal Party MP called Cyril Smith and that has always been my personal definition of over-crowding.)

Adolf liked to belittle his staff and once ordered a senior editor on the paper where he was the boss to telephone me to find out how to spell a word in an article someone else had written. It was a pure example of power. I sent a message back that I would buy the editor a dictionary if he didn't have one. He died a few years ago and I don't know how many there were at his funeral but I doubt if many of those there were in mourning. Most of those present probably turned up just to make sure he was dead.

Anyway, Adolf and I sat down in the dining room and a waiter brought two menus and greeted me by name but ignored the editor.

Slightly puzzled and a trifle put out, the editor looked up and then studied his menu, no doubt looking for something packed with the greatest possible number of calories.

A moment later another waiter came over, solely to say hello and to ask how I was.

And then a third came over and greeted me. This time it was the head waiter. He shook me by the hand.

And then the wine waiter came over, spoke to me by name and asked how I was.

The editor, now finding it impossible not to look impressed, glared at me as though I had organised some sort of practical joke.

It was one of those glorious few minutes that don't occur often enough in life. What the editor didn't know (and what I hadn't bothered to tell him before we'd arrived) was that for several years I had always stayed at The Ritz when I had to be in London.

Adolf had picked the one hotel in London where this was likely to happen.

None of this did my contract negotiations any harm at all.

And it made up for the 7,329 times in my life when I felt gauche and rather too much like a hapless country yokel and only thought of the clever thing to do or say a minute or so too late.

The Magician

I did so much television work that for a while in the 1980s I was a member of Equity, the actors' union. The highlight of my membership was the evening when I helped out a friend and worked as a magician's assistant. My job was to hand the magician the props he needed, and although I was wearing the clothes I'd turned up in (sports jacket and flannels as I remember) and would not have fit the usual idea of a magician's assistant (fishnet tights, lots of sparkle and plenty of bosom) I was the only person available because it was a union gig (which is to say that everyone appearing on stage had to be in Equity) and I was the only spare body present with a union card.

The main trick of the performance was the traditional sawing in half of a lady. The magician duly selected a volunteer from the audience; a lady who was well built in all departments and who had clearly fortified herself before the event with something stronger than a nice cup of tea.

The magician, who was blessed with plenty of patter and panache but not a great deal of the skills usually required of a magician, rather relied on the audience being some distance away so that the occasional fumble went unnoticed (the clumsiness of approaching old age perhaps explains why he had accepted me as his assistant). He used an electric power saw to do the cutting and when I saw how the trick worked (I was standing two feet away and could hardly not see the secret) I was terrified and very relieved when the plump lady volunteer could finally clamber off the stage and wobble back to her seat, basking in the applause.

I'm not going to tell you the secret, of course…

…oh, damnit, yes I am.

Magicians spill the beans all the time and I was never anywhere near the Magic Circle. Besides most people probably know how it works so I'm not giving much away. And I never said I wouldn't. And the magician long ago took a permanent gig working in an arena where every trick works perfectly and only the clouds are fluffy.

You have to remember, by the way, that this was a simple cutting in half. There was no question of hands wiggling from one cube, feet jiggling at the bottom of another cube and a smiling face poking out of the third cube. This was a very simple, old-fashioned sawing in half.

The saw (in this case an electric saw) consisted of a long saw-toothed blade attached to an ordinary Black and Decker type of power tool and it looked terrifying – more like one of those power tools used to trim hedges than anything else.

The volunteer to be cut in half lay down on a couch (in our case a folding couch of the variety favoured by travelling physiotherapists and masseurs) and after a frame work had been laid over the her midriff (one of my tasks had been to find her a glass of water to help banish her hiccups) the magician held up the saw and pressed the trigger to show everyone that it worked. He then clicked the saw into position at one side of the framework (which was fitted with sides ostensibly to stop the blood flying everywhere but in reality to ensure that the audience couldn't see too much) and proceeded to move the saw across to the other side of the frame in order to cut the woman in half.

When the saw reached the far side of the woman, with the motor running all the time, the magician unclipped it from the framework and held it up high, keeping his finger on the trigger all the time so that we could still hear the motor running and could see that the blade was moving.

The trick lay, of course, in the fact that there were two blades.

When the saw was placed in the frame, the first blade was automatically disconnected from the electric drill part of the assembly. The magician kept the saw buzzing but there was, by now, no blade attached. When the drill, with buzzing motor, reached the far side of the woman's midriff, it automatically reconnected with a second blade. And when the magician held up the saw, the vibrating blade could be seen to be working.

It was a decent trick, though spoilt a little by the fact that the magician had something of a tremor and wasn't as strong as he had once been, with the result that there was a rather lengthy delay while he managed to make sure that the saw connected with the second blade before he held it up for the audience to see. I suspect, too, that the connectors were a little worn and didn't work quite as well as they once had.

And there was something else too and this was entirely my fault.

When, a few moments before the performance, the magician had done a quick rehearsal of the equipment I had seen how the trick worked.

'You could put some tomato ketchup on the second blade,' I said. 'So when you hold it up to the audience they'll think they can see blood dripping from it.'

The suggestion was made as a joke. But the magician thought it a great idea and sent me off to the theatre's restaurant to fetch a bottle of tomato ketchup. Together we then poured a liberal quantity of tomato ketchup over the blade.

We should have tried it before the performance. Neither of us realised just how much ketchup will fly off a saw blade which is being operated by an electric motor. The stuff went everywhere. It covered the magician's one and only sparkly purple outfit. A misty cloud of it sprayed as far as the front row of the audience – most of whom screamed in what sounded to me like genuine horror. And a good deal of it went over the posh frock worn by the plump volunteer still lying on the folding couch table.

Her husband, as luck would have it, turned out to be a solicitor (one who specialised in conveyancing but a solicitor nevertheless, and a solicitor is a solicitor is a solicitor as Gertrude Stein probably said whenever she was sued) and he demanded £100 to cover the cost of a new frock. After some bargaining we got this down to £50 in cash. And since the tomato ketchup had been my idea I agreed to go halves with the magician.

In the end we couldn't even raise £50 in cash and we gave her £37.50. The magician gave her £22 and the £15.50 was my contribution.

Since I didn't get paid for the gig this means that my one and only performance as a magician's assistant (and a professional, unionised one at that) cost me £15.50.

Mickey Spillane

Publishers, editors, literary agents and literary editors have always been a snooty lot. The majority of them wanted to be authors but were hindered by their inability to put an interesting sentence together. If someone had offered them a sack of gold tied up with a pink ribbon they wouldn't have been able to put together anything more fun to read than someone else's bank statement. And so, in addition to being snooty, the publishing professionals hate authors.

Actually, they hate authors for three reasons.

First, they are jealous.

Second, they depend on them.

And, thirdly, they hate authors whose books are successful (and make money) because they want to be able to do that but can't – and because they depend upon those sales to survive. Publishers make far more fuss of academic authors than of commercial authors. And newspapers such as *The Guardian* give most of their review space to books that no one will ever buy, let alone read. (*The Guardian* serialised my first book *The Medicine Men* and the book got huge review space. We all knew it was never going to be a bestseller though it did well enough and large stacks of it were displayed on railway station bookstalls which surprised and delighted me. *The Guardian* gave my second book, *Paper Doctors* a great review. But after that, when my books started to sell in decent quantities, *The Guardian* only ever mentioned me and my books to be rude about us.)

Sadly, most traditional publishers are also stupid and unimaginative and depend on marketing men and women (the highly paid folk in Italian silk suits who run the publishing industry) to tell them what to publish. And so they allow themselves to look forever backwards rather than forwards; generally favouring the tried and successful over the imaginative and the challenging.

The marketing 'suits' look to see what sold well last year and instruct editors to find and publish more of the same. If a book on cooking Indian food did well last year then the publishers will, in two years' time, flood the market with books on Indian food. If a rather coy novel set in the Home Counties climbs into the bestseller lists, there will be a flood of entirely similar novels on the stocks for the next few years.

None of this matters terribly much because most publishing houses exist within media conglomerates. The book publishers exist to provide copy for magazine, newspaper and television studios. And even if they were run more sensibly, book publishers would never make a profit because they invariably end up paying out huge advances to political figures who are owed a favour.

(How this works is simple. The politician (let's call him Tony Blair, just because that's a name) who has done favours for the conglomerate's owners, will be given an advance of, say £5 million even though everyone in the world knows that the book will never sell enough copies to cover the cost of the advance. The money is, in reality, paid out as a reward for services rendered.)

I do not, by the way, offer these criticisms out of bitterness. I did well enough through London publishers but eventually found self-publishing far more satisfying, both artistically and commercially.

Just about every publisher in London rejected the MSS of my book *Alice's Diary*, claiming snootily that there was absolutely no market for a book allegedly written by a cat. I published it myself and sold 60,000 hardback copies in the first year. (That would have put the book at or near the top of the bestseller lists for many weeks.)

I offer these random and seemingly irrelevant thoughts only as introduction to one of my favourite literary anecdotes.

Way back, in the mid part of the last century, a new young writer called Mickey Spillane started writing hard-boiled novels about a private eye called Mike Hammer. Spillane's style was raw and tough and relentless and about as politically incorrect as you could get. Mike Hammer was twice as tough as Philip Marlow and Sam Spade put together.

Spillane's books sold by the container load. No one had ever sold as many books in such a short space of time. Indeed, no one had ever sold as many books.

After a few years of success, Spillane was at a literary event in New York when another party goer, a publisher, approached him.

'I see that of the top ten bestselling books of all time, seven are yours,' said the snooty partygoer, clearly appalled. 'I think it's awful,' he added, in case there had been any doubt in Spillane's mind. (The other three books in the all-time ten top selling books at the time included *The Bible*, Dr Benjamin Spock's book on child care and a novel by Jacqueline Susann called *Valley of the Dolls*.)

'You should think yourself lucky that I've only written seven books,' replied Spillane, never a man to take a sneer lying down.

You have to love a man who thinks like that.

Spillane, incidentally, was a good egg. He was a Jehovah's Witness who loved animals. He bought a huge farm so that the wildlife could run free without any interference from hunters or farmers or men from the Government. It was, I suppose, the first 're-wilding' project, though, although I was never fortunate enough to meet him, I suspect that Spillane wouldn't have wanted to have anything to with anything quite so absurdly politically correct.

Literary Agents

I no longer have a literary agent in the UK (though I have active and enthusiastic agents in other countries around the world) and I don't expect I'll ever have a UK agent again. Over the decades, my criticism of government lies and propaganda means that I have become persona non grata with all aspects of the mainstream publishing industry in the UK. It's odd, really. You'd think they'd welcome truths and original thinking. But, sadly, no mainstream publisher will consider my books, no mainstream newspaper or magazine editor will publish reviews of my books (let alone publish articles by me) and no mainstream broadcaster would dream of letting me into a studio.

I no longer give a damn.

But, like most professional authors, I have over the years employed a number of literary agents to represent me, to find publishers, occasionally to put me in touch with editors who had an idea for a book and needed an experienced author to write it, to sell books abroad and to negotiate serial rights, translation rights and other rights. In what I now think of as the first third of what might laughingly be called my career, I had a couple of literary agents.

When I first started writing (and before I became a full-time author in my early 30s) it was customary for all authors to have agents. The process of turning an idea into a saleable item went through many stages and, often, many years. The author would take an idea or a synopsis or a few chapters of a book to an agent. The agent would offer it to publishers (either in parallel or in series according to the perceived value of the product) who would consult with their marketing men before considering making an offer. If bought, written and published, the finished book would then be offered to bookshop buyers and touted to reviewers before getting anywhere near a real reader. The road to success was a long and stony one.

For a couple of decades (the last two thirds of my career) I have published my own books.

For one half of that two thirds, I published hard and paperback editions and had offices, a warehouse and a distribution centre known, rather grandly, as Publishing House. I remember an ageing and sanctimonious journalist hired by the *Sunday Telegraph* once asking me how I decided what to write. I told her that I just wrote books I wanted to write and then presented them to potential readers who, I hoped, would buy enough copies to make each book commercially viable.

She was appalled. 'Isn't that rather self-indulgent?' she demanded, apparently failing to understand anything about books. And maybe she wasn't a very good journalist either because the long feature she was hired to write never saw the light of day. She must have had a good appetite, though for there was a great deal of her. If a fit man walked around her he would have needed to sit down afterwards to get his breath back.

In recent years I gave up running my own proper publishing house. The retirement of several long-standing employees triggered the thought that I was a little old to be lugging around heavy boxes of books and fighting the Royal Mail, the printers and staff problems. More and more publishers were moving to digital printing and the cost of traditional printing was rising rapidly.

Industries which are near the end of their lives always make the same mistake as printers seemed to be making. I'm sure that as the demand for buggy whips fell away, the buggy whip manufacturers attempted to deal with their falling income by putting up the price of their whips – thereby speeding up their demise.

Today all my books are sold through online – usually as both paperbacks and eBooks. I just write the books and publish them. Someone else puts the books in cardboard envelopes and deals with the problem of moving them from here to there or from there to here. And someone else deals with the mechanics of the digital printing process. Originally, I had grave doubts about the security of eBooks and I have had a number of books stolen and sold by other people but no one with any sense would do things any other way. Some of my books are sold to libraries and bookshops and the English language editions are sold around the world. I keep foreign language rights and sell those direct to publishers in other countries.

I fear that traditional publishers are doomed and the only need for literary agents is to offer books to be translated into other languages.

Back when I started, however, a literary agent was essential.

My first agent, Anne McDermid, worked then for an agency called David Higham in Golden Square, London and she found me, rather than the other way around. I was still in my early 20s at the time, and she saw an article of mine in, I think, the *Daily Telegraph* and wrote and asked if I would like to turn the idea into a book. She knew my parents' address because she was related to a near neighbour of theirs.

The book that resulted was called *The Medicine Men* and was published by a marvellous old world publisher called Maurice Temple-Smith whose eponymous firm was headquartered in an office about the size of a newspaper kiosk situated, fashionably, across from the British Museum and a few yards away from a famous magic shop where performers such as Tommy Cooper used to purchase tricks, or go to have tricks made for them.

Maurice published my first three non-fiction books. *The Medicine Men*, *Paper Doctors* and *Stress Control*, and we both did well with them. They all had fantastic reviews and the first and third were bought by mass market paperback houses. Copies were racked up in stacks on railway station bookstalls and in branches of W.H.Smith; a store which was, in those days, essential to authors. *Stress Control* was the first mass market book about stress and it sold quite decently.

I was told then that the buyer for Smiths was reputed to order books on the basis of their covers alone (hence the garish and colourful covers that publishers selected). I was also assured that if a book wasn't selling quickly enough, the copies would be put in a box and returned to the unfortunate publisher within days of their arrival.

Actually, I say we did well with those books but financially, *The Medicine Men* wasn't a great success. There was a sale to a book club and a couple of foreign sales in addition to the paperback but the cost of having the manuscript retyped and then libel read came to around twice the money I initially received for writing it. Still, it didn't lose money. In those days an author usually received an advance against the expected sales. The first third was paid on signature of the contract. The second third was paid on delivery of an acceptable typescript. And the final third was paid on publication. I have no idea what the custom is these days.

I stayed with Miss McDermid for quite a while and moved with her when she went to work at another well-known agency, Curtis Brown, which had offices in Regent Street. She sold quite a few books for me and the overseas department sold foreign rights around the world. The TV department fixed me with some TV presenting work too, though I never felt comfortable in front of a camera and wasn't much good at it.

I wanted to write polemics, like the books I'd written for Maurice Temple-Smith, who had long retired, and Anne grew tired of this. I suspect that she wanted me to write the sort of thing packagers such as Dorling Kindersley produce – mass market books where the words fight for space alongside loads of pretty pictures. These packaged books were all the rage in the 1970s and 1980s because once they had been designed, the words could be translated and different versions slotted in among the illustrations. I did a few of these and fell out when, after writing four books in one heavily illustrated series, an editor told me that I had to extol the virtues of meat eating in a book about food because otherwise the publishers of the German edition would be unhappy. As a vegetarian I refused and the series ended abruptly. I bought back the book I'd written and published it myself as *Food for Thought*. It sold well and I managed to sell quite a few lots of foreign rights. Actually, the book still sells well though if it had remained as part of a series of packaged books it would have died years ago – that's what happened to the other books in the series. That's another thing about mainstream publishers. They never think about the long-term; they never think about creating a viable backlist. They're always looking for something to sell for a few months and to then be discarded. Just about everything I ever self-published is still in print and still earning me an income.

Anne and I had a few big successes together (*Bodypower* and *Life without Tranquillisers* were both in all the bestseller lists, though initially it was difficult to get publishers to take an interest in either book) but eventually I received a rather short letter (in both senses) complaining that I was becoming a 'prophet crying in the wilderness' and suggesting, I seem to remember, that I become a little more commercial or find another agent.

Word got around London that I was without an agent and several people approached me. The one I liked best was a former editor called Darley Anderson who had published quite a few of my books at a publisher called Sheldon Press and had done well enough with them. He definitely understood the value of building up a backlist.

Darley invited me to be his first author since he was leaving Sheldon Press to set up his own literary agency.

But within a week or two, before I'd signed any agreement, I made what was probably the worst mistake of my professional career as an author.

A friend of mine, a publisher and author, came to stay for the weekend with his girlfriend. She too was setting up as an agent and they pressured me all weekend to sign with her. Foolishly I succumbed to their promises – though mainly I succumbed because I felt too embarrassed to say 'no' after all their pressure.

Darley went on to become one of London's most successful agents (his client list included Lee Child, author of the Jack Reacher series) and my relationship with my new agent quickly went wrong when it became clear that she wanted to tell me which books to write and which not to write. I've never been much good at doing what I'm told to do, and never been any good at all at writing to order. To be honest, I can't see the point – unless you're just writing for money.

And that was that as far as agents are concerned.

I did talk to one or two other agents but we never hit it off. One unpleasant fellow had just set up an agency and was very interested in handling my Fleet Street work, promising that he could get me more money from the paper I was working for. He was a strangely unprepossessing fellow. He wore a misshapen suit which looked like a grey dustcover thrown over an unusually shaped piece of furniture. His hair was interesting, too. It looked as though it had been cut in one of those places where they advertise free haircuts if you let a student do the snipping. And he'd obviously got the blind student they'd taken on in order to get some sort of grant.

Since I'd just signed a new six figure contract (of which he would get ten per cent) I could understand his enthusiasm but I'd been dealing with Fleet Street long enough to know he wouldn't be able to do any better than I had. He was a smarmy fellow, far too pleased with himself, who had too much of an air of a second-hand car dealer about him to be of any use – either with book publishers or with newspaper editors. He reeked of a very unpleasant and potent aftershave which would, I suspect, have been useful for keeping foxes out of the garden. Looking him up the other day, he seems to have been as singularly unsuccessful as I would have expected him to be.

And he was the end of my association with the orthodox publishing within the UK. A few publishers wrote asking me to do books with them but by then I was too enchanted with the idea of publishing my own books to be interested.

Literary agents still seem to think they are essential but they're as outdated as typewriters with ribbons and, despite their bravado and constant assertions of importance, they'll fade away quite quickly now. They are, to put it simply, beyond their sell by date.

Circus Clowns

'One of the last of the Fratellini family of clowns, an old man, made a television address in Paris a few years ago in which he blamed (child labour laws and compulsory education) for the dearth of good, young circus clowns. 'When I was a child, my father, bless him, broke my legs so that I would walk comically, as a clown should,' the old man said. 'Now there are people who would take a poor view of such a thing.''
From 'Between Meals: An Appetite for Paris', A.J.Liebling, 1959.
(If you have not read this book, then I heartily recommend Liebling – an astonishingly nutritious author.)

Cars

My very first car was an old Humber Super Snipe which I purchased for £30 when I was a medical student. As I drove it away from the garage it was raining. When I turned on the wipers they both flew off into the middle of the road, never to be seen again. The car had no MOT and I don't remember ever having a tax disk for it. It did four miles to the gallon and unless I parked it on a hill I needed the RAC to help me get it to start. They were surprisingly sympathetic and never seemed upset. Eventually, I took it back to the salesman, who operated on a bombed site close to the centre of Birmingham, and he happily swapped it for an old Ford van which was much more reliable though it had a few faults of its own. The van was so rotten that on my first journey the whole back end of the bodywork fell off and landed on the road behind me. The front of the car couldn't have been much better because I remember putting my foot through the floor. Quite a large hole developed and it was slightly alarming to see the road whizzing past beneath you. The steering wheel used to come off if I pulled on it and the handbrake came away too if I pulled too hard. If we were travelling on a nice straight piece of road, I used to hand the steering wheel to passengers and ask them if they'd like to drive.

The little Ford van was surprisingly reliable for a while but eventually, not even the RAC could make it go and I abandoned it in the multi storey car park next to the Birmingham General Hospital. I subsequently received a letter demanding that I pay £50 to have it taken away. That, of course, was more than it had cost me when I'd bought it.

For a while I walked or used trains and then, when I was a young GP in the early 1970s, I acquired an old wooden sided Mini Traveller which had belonged to my mother. I liked the car. It was one of those with the wooden bits on the side, but there were a few problems with it. First and foremost I found that getting in and out of the car many times a day wasn't doing my back any good. Second, I climbed in and out of it so much that one of the hinges holding the driver's door in place broke, leaving the door hanging by the hinge that was left. Third, the car didn't much like starting in cold weather. Actually it didn't much like starting in warm weather either.

I had a lot of fun with it though, and it survived a fairly hefty crash with a van which came from the left on a roundabout and did quite a lot of damage to the front and nearside. I left the car with a nearby garage and rented something which, apart from the wheels, appeared to have been made entirely out of plastic.

When I went to collect the Mini Traveller, the garage didn't want to let me take the car away unless I paid their bill in cash. Since the bill was substantial, I didn't have enough money on me and offered them a cheque. They refused the cheque and insisted that I go away and return with cash.

'I need to test drive it first,' I said to the boss.

'OK,' he said. 'But I'm coming with you.'

We both climbed into the car and I drove for three or four miles before pulling into the kerb.

'It seems fine,' I said. 'If you accept a cheque I'll drive you back to your garage. If you won't take a cheque you can either come with me or get out and walk back to your garage.'

He looked cross for a moment and then grinned. 'I didn't see that coming,' he confessed. He took the cheque and I drove him back to the garage.

After that crash I decided I wanted a slightly larger, more substantial vehicle. The nearest garage to where I lived was a specialist Saab dealer, and so I popped along there to have a look at what they'd got on offer. Buying a car from a garage with a dealer less than half a mile away made sense. The only model the dealer had in stock was a brand new Saab 99 in bright orange. At the time, Saab had a reputation for making solid cars.

'It's much safer than anything else on the road,' the dealer pointed out. 'People can see you coming from miles away. And you'll be able to find it easily in a car park.'

I hummed and hawed for a few minutes, wrote out a cheque and drove the car home.

I kept the Saab for two or three years and when it came time to buy something else I went back to the dealer to see if he'd buy it from me.

'It's a terrible colour,' said the dealer. 'I'll have a job to sell it to anyone. Who wants a bright orange car?'

'You told me it would be safer and easier to find in a car park,' I pointed out.

The dealer grinned. 'Well, I had to sell the damned thing to someone,' he said. 'I'd had it in the showroom for weeks. No one wanted it because of the colour.'

'But you said it was a lovely colour!' I reminded him.

'So I did,' the dealer agreed. 'But that was when I was selling. Now that I'm buying it's a terrible, bloody colour. No one will want to buy it unless I can offer it very cheap.'

So I learnt a valuable lesson.

Buying and selling are two entirely different things.

My next car was a brown Volvo estate.

And I'll tell you something: even with the permanent riding lights (which could only be switched off if you removed a fuse) other motorists never seemed to see it at all, particularly in poor light or bad weather.

And I could never find the damned thing in car parks.

The Big Sleep

Any fan of Humphrey Bogart who has ever watched the classic movie *The Big Sleep* will remember that the plot is sometimes difficult to follow.

Those who feel that they are confused because they haven't been paying attention should know that when the film of Raymond Chandler's novel was being made, Humphrey Bogart who was playing private detective Philip Marlowe, suddenly asked the director, Howard Hawks, which of the other characters had killed someone called Geiger who was a chauffeur and who had been found shot at one point in the movie.

Hawks realised that he didn't know who was responsible so he asked William Faulkner, who was the script writer.

Faulkner confessed that he didn't know, so he telephoned Raymond Chandler to ask him if he could explain who had killed Geiger.

Chandler thought for a few moments and then quietly confessed that he didn't have the foggiest.

So, there you are: anyone who claims to understand what is going on in *The Big Sleep* is full of duck shit. The film (like the book) has such a convoluted plot that no one really understands what is going on. Just enjoy Bogart.

Police Surgeon

When I worked as a GP one of my partners was the local police surgeon. And the deal was that in return for his sharing the annual fee among the five partners, we would act as his understudies when it was our turn to be on call at night, weekends and bank holidays (in those days it was customary for GPs to be available for house calls 24 hours a day and 365 days a year). We were, in effect, alternate police surgeons. Some of the things I experienced in that job would, these days, require a lifetime of counselling.

Most of the time the work was routine; with much of it involving taking blood samples from motorists who were suspected of driving under the influence of alcohol. I remember that drivers could give a urine sample or a blood sample and the local coroner got rather caught out by the urine test. Being something of an enthusiastic toper, particularly at lunchtime, he reckoned that he would get round the test by keeping a small sample bottle of urine in his car. The sample was regularly replaced by a pal of his who was another local GP and who simply handed him part of a sample provided by a patient.

When the coroner was stopped one afternoon, on his way home from a largely liquid luncheon paid for by a drug company, he took his urine bottle into the loo with him and switched it for the official bottle he'd been given. This is a genuine story but you can probably guess the rest.

'Was my sample OK?' he later asked my partner the police surgeon.

'It was fine,' he was told. 'No alcohol. But you need to see your own doctor. The sample shows that you're diabetic and you're pregnant.'

Fortunately, the coroner saw the funny side of it. He'd been deliberately scammed by the doctor who'd provided him with the sample.

The coroner was a genial old fellow who had spent many years practising the art of loafing. All the practice he'd had, together with the appropriate genetic predisposition, meant that he was very, very good at doing almost nothing. He was a bachelor and he contrived to get himself invited to all the drug company luncheons and dinners. It was said in the town that he had eaten out twice a day for at least a decade and never once paid for a meal or a drink. Only at weekends did he have to fend for himself, and then he ate in one of the local pubs where he and the restaurant manager had an 'understanding' which meant that his wallet remained in his jacket pocket. (I am assured that if you are in the licensed trade, it is never a bad idea to keep in with someone who is an important figure in the local judiciary.)

Whenever I was standing in for the police surgeon, I usually found taking blood samples from drivers to be an incredibly sad business. Most of the motorists who had been stopped were well aware of the trouble they were in and had sobered up a good deal by the time I saw them. They could see themselves losing their jobs and homes as well as their driving licences. And the local paper was merciless in reporting their shame. Some of the motorists I saw were my patients and were either embarrassed or wanted me to let them off. My sympathy was limited, however. When I'd worked in hospital casualty units I'd seen plenty of people who had been injured in car crashes caused by drunken drivers.

Occasionally, there were motorists who were aggressive, threatening or just plain difficult. One young driver, who appeared to have been built using the blueprints for a 1970s office block, and who was so obviously drunk that taking blood was a formality, refused to allow me to take blood from his arm and insisted instead that I took it from his penis. He unzipped his trousers and produced the item in question. I asked the station sergeant for a piece of paper, wrote a few lines of formal prose, handed the paper to the drunken driver and asked him to sign it.

The conversation went like this.

'What's this? What do you want me to sign?'

'It's a release form.'

'What do you mean? Release from what?'

'If I take blood from your penis there are additional risks. I need you to sign to accept that you're willing to accept the risk.'

'What sort of risks?'

'Taking blood from your penis may make it shrivel up. It may even fall off.'

'It's not very big to start with, mate!' said the sergeant, helpfully. 'You wouldn't want it any smaller.'

The driver looked down and then stared at me in disbelief. 'I'm not signing that!' he said, pushing the piece of paper back at me, hastily putting his penis back into hiding and zipping up his trousers. He took off his jacket, rolled up his shirt sleeve, offered me his arm and demanded that I took blood from there as though it had been me who'd suggested taking blood from his penis.

I had a few people try the same trick. But they were all easily dissuaded.

Those were the easy, bread and butter calls.

More straightforward, for example, than the time I was called to examine a large plastic bag which the dustmen had found too heavy to lift into their cart and regarded as 'suspicious looking'. They were right to be suspicions. After poking a hole through the plastic I could see a hand and then an ear.

It turned out that the occupier of the house had, after murdering his wife, stuffed her into a plastic bag and left her outside on the pavement with the used bottles and other household detritus. The policeman in charge didn't want me to unwrap the parcel and we had quite a row. I pointed out that until I'd unwrapped enough of the parcel to perform some sort of examination, I couldn't confirm that the body belonged to a dead person. And until I certified that the body was dead, the police couldn't do anything.

I remember once being called out in the middle of the night to certify the death of a man who had been murdered by burglars. The burglars had even killed the man's dog – using a poker on both man and dog. After I'd certified the man as dead, the policeman in charge pompously told me that I could go because they would prefer to await the arrival of a proper forensic pathologist to do the technical stuff.

I happily went home and was called two hours later and asked to return. It turned out that every forensic pathologist in the country was attending their annual dinner a hundred miles away. So would I please go back? I went back and spent hours taking the temperatures of both the dead man and his dog and doing everything else that I could imagine a forensic pathologist might do. The police caught the two culprits a day or so later, and I had to examine and take hair and nail samples from them both. They were a typical folie a deux. One of the murderers was nasty and unconcerned and the other rather simple minded and tearful. I remember having a row that time too. The police didn't want to leave me alone with either of the arrested men but as far as I was concerned they were patients and I was the doctor. I wasn't having policemen in the room while I performed my examinations. I knew I was perfectly safe because there wasn't a poker in the room. Besides, I felt content that no criminal was going to feel boisterous when I'd got a pair of scissors in my hand and was taking pubic hair samples.

And there was the time that I got a call to visit a woman who was seriously mentally ill. She had told a neighbour that she had made a cake for all her friends and neighbours and had put into the cake mix every tablet she'd been given. Since she was seriously psychotic and had been given a fairly large supply of heavy duty pills, I found this slightly alarming. She told me she had put the whole lot into the cake. I had to ask the local police force to visit everyone to whom she'd given a piece of the cake and to retrieve every slice. One man had put his slice into his briefcase and taken it with him to London. We got them all back though and when we fitted every slice together, we could see that we'd retrieved the whole cake.

And then there was the vet who shot himself with the sort of bolt gun used to put down large animals, and the man who burnt to death in a house fire which was so intense that all that remained was a blackened skeleton. I could smell the burnt flesh from half a mile away and I could still smell it weeks later.

But you don't want to hear about those.

Duncan

He built his life on a foundation of lies and self-deceits, piled high, one upon the other, but, by and large, he was the only victim of his mendacity. He remembered things that had never happened and dreamt of things that never would. His whole existence was built upon disappointments, frustrations and recriminations, some of which were real but many of which were imagined.

When I first met him he was a young, well-known local radio presenter with his own daily show on one of the BBC's local radio stations. I was the radio doctor for four or five local radio stations – and a dozen or so more who syndicated a couple of the shows – and his was one of the stations where I worked. They paid me what is usually called an honorarium (which meant that it just about covered my expenses) and I did the shows because I thought that they might provide the listeners with useful information and eventually help me sell some books.

Duncan had only been on air a short while but he had already acquired hundreds of thousands of faithful listeners. He had a simple, rather cocky style on air which made him sound like everybody's favourite son, grandson or nephew; always a little bit cheeky, always promising more than he could possibly give, always about to get into serious trouble but always able to slide away from the problems he seemed destined to encounter. If he'd been a car salesman he'd have sold second-hand cars off a bombed site. In London, he'd have made a good living selling slightly unfashionable china off a stall in Petticoat lane. Or, perhaps, selling stockings from out of a suitcase and running like the wind if one of his look-outs shouted 'Copper!'.

The first thing I noticed about him was that he always smiled when he was working on air. It was a cheekie chappie sort of smile, and I knew immediately that the listeners could hear the smile in his voice. It was the smile they couldn't see that gave him the charm. He'd been a professional photographer for a while and you could easily imagine him coaxing his subjects to do a little or this or a little of that. He'd have been marvellous with the bride, the groom and the wedding guests. He was one of the few professional broadcasters I've met, and over the year I've met many hundreds, who was the same person behind a microphone as he was talking in the corridor outside the studio or chatting in the pub down the road.

The thing that the listeners didn't hear in his voice was the lack of confidence, the fear of imminent failure and the suspicion that the world was always about to make him pay for the good fortune which had taken him from a job selling carpet squares and rugs ('the insurance company classified them as water damaged, which is how we can sell them at a fraction of the usual price, but if you can find anything to complain about I'll give you your money back with a bottle of wine thrown in') to a gig on local radio. He'd worked for a while doing a once a week show on the local hospital radio station ('and this one is for Mr Watson who has just has his gall bladder removed') and he'd done a daily late night show on a small commercial station. And finally he'd risen to having his own morning show on a bigger radio station in the centre of a large city. He was almost good enough to be on national radio but he didn't have the confidence, the contacts, the cockiness or the ruthlessness required to take that final step upwards.

Radio presenters didn't get paid much in those days, the station paid him less for three hours a day and two hours on Sunday mornings than the owner of the carpet shop had paid him. But he was in show business and there were more perks in radio than there ever were in selling water damaged rugs. Once or twice a week he'd be paid to open a shop or play records at a birthday party or an anniversary 'do'. He'd be paid fifty or a hundred quid in cash, though he admitted he would have done it for nothing, just for the joy of signing a few autographs and posing for photos.

He loved posing for photos with fans.

Mobile phones didn't have cameras in those days and the selfie hadn't been invented but he'd pose for two or three pictures with his arm round the birthday 'girl'. She was always somewhere between the age of 40 and 100. The ones at the younger end of that range would sometimes pinch his bum and slip him a piece of paper with their name, phone number and address scribbled on it.

He told me once that a woman listener had invited him to go round for afternoon tea. He'd responded to the promise in her voice and turned up to find her waiting for him naked except for a pair of high heeled shoes. Later she boasted to him that she'd slept with nearly all of the station's male presenters and all but three of the on air female presenters. He never did get a cup of tea, though.

I've been on thousands of radio programmes and Duncan was one of the very best of all the local radio presenters I've met. He had a distinctive, friendly style which was ideally suited to community radio and he a few clever tricks of his own. He would sit in the studio with a copy of the local A to Z on the desk in front of him and when he spoke to a caller he would ask them where they lived. While chatting, he would then look up the name of their street in the A to Z, pretend to think for a moment and then, using the map, talk to them about all the local landmarks – schools, pubs, parks, shopping centres and churches. Callers loved him. And at the time, although I'd been to radio stations everywhere, I'd never seen anyone else do this. Added to a natural charm and easy manner it made him a perfect local radio presenter. The listeners felt that he knew them, their neighbourhood and their lives. He soon acquired quite a reputation as the man who knew the city best.

And then, although his ratings were excellent, the programme manager decided that a double headed show would do better and that a woman presenter should sit alongside him. And so a far less talented, acid-tongued female presenter joined him and she broke the spell.

For a quick laugh, and the chance to put him down, she told the listeners his secret.

'He just sits here with an A to Z in front of him,' she scoffed. 'He doesn't really know where your park is or the name of the nearest church.'

For a quick, two second put-down she had destroyed him.

It wasn't so much that his harmless trick was exposed as that the listeners were encouraged to believe that he'd been lying to them and that they'd been cheated.

Duncan was appalled. He was broken. He felt shamed and betrayed. He'd never been able to manage internal office politics. He was more sensitive than those working with him believed him to be. He didn't have the self-confidence or the courage to cope. He had a decent sized ego but it was fragile. The woman's nasty comment wrecked his fragile self-confidence.

I wasn't surprised by what happened.

I knew many BBC radio stations quite well.

Unlike the commercial stations, which tended to be bright and full of quick thinking, go-ahead people, the BBC stations were miserable, dowdy places: full of intrigue and political nonsenses.

It is often said that the BBC is the voice of the left-leaning political establishment. It isn't. The BBC is the voice of the State. Since the BBC runs all its staff recruitment advertising in *The Guardian* newspaper this is not particularly surprising. It has always surprised me that a national organisation should be allowed to recruit exclusively from a relatively tiny band of heavy breathing pantywaisters and buttinskis who are eager to represent and promote the State.

Suddenly, without thinking about it, Duncan announced that he was leaving.

He had, he said, been offered work in America. He was emigrating to find fame and fortune in a bigger market. On the radio he spoke about the fantastic job he'd been offered.

There were the usual words of congratulation from others working at the station.

One or two were doubtless pleased for him. Some were sad to see him go. More than a few were slightly green with envy at the sound of the fantastic job he'd somehow managed to land. He said he'd been hired because of his English accent.

Since I knew him well, and appeared regularly on his programme, his producer asked if I would telephone and wish him goodbye during his final show. I said I would do better than that. I drove 200 miles from Devon, where I lived at the time, and when I arrived at the Pebble Mill Studios in Birmingham I telephoned the studio on a pay phone (there were no mobile telephones in those days). I wished him well and then pretended that I really wanted to be there with him in person.

'The show finishes in 30 minutes,' he said sadly. 'You'll never get here from Devon.'

I promised him that I'd make it. I ran up the stairs and two minutes later I bounced into the studio.

After the show had finished we went for coffee and promised to keep in touch.

He rang me the next day.

He was in Exmouth in Devon.

He was staying at his parents' home. He hadn't gone to America. There had never been any job there. He had resigned without anywhere to go. He was unemployed. He wanted to know if I could find him some work. His mouth still smiled but his eyes were dead. Not surprisingly, perhaps, I never saw them smile again. His face had once radiated hope. His eyes had genuinely twinkled. He enjoyed entertaining people. The face which had once radiated hope and ambition now radiated defeat and despair. Hope and ambition had been cruelly displaced by despair and failure.

He desperately needed something to do, and a little money. He needed to be useful. He asked me if I could find him some work. He offered to do some gardening. I hired him to knock down an old greenhouse which had rotten frames and broken glass. He did that for a while but it was clear he just wanted the company.

I knew people at the BBC in Devon and at the commercial radio station in Exeter and I arranged for him to work first at one and then at the other. A friend, another disc jockey, found him occasional work at a popular English speaking radio station operating in Vienna. He was given a good contract, found decent accommodation and paid well.

But he had started drinking heavily.

He turned up late for shows or didn't turn up at all. He went on air slurring his words.

In the world of radio these are unforgiveable sins.

He was fired, fired and fired again; fired from at least three radio stations. I was cross with him for letting himself down, and for embarrassing me, but our friendship survived.

He took a job as a salesman, hired to sell time share apartments but couldn't bear the idea of tricking gullible customers and he never sold anything. He told potential customers all the flaws, all the problems, all the reasons why they shouldn't spend their money on a time share apartment. This showed a sense of morality above and beyond his duty to himself for he was due to be paid only when he sold something. His determined honesty meant that he didn't sell a single time share apartment and, after a few weeks, left no richer than he'd been when he'd started the job.

Then he managed to get a job as a photographer on a local paper in Worcestershire. This wasn't surprising for, as I've mentioned, he'd been a professional photographer before he'd started broadcasting.

But he didn't stop drinking. He drank more and more. He took blurry photographs at a couple of weddings.

He refused all offers of help. He said his drinking wasn't a problem. I spoke to him regularly but he shouted at me when I tried to persuade him to get help. At one point he boasted that he'd found a way to make money. He bought new cameras, insured them, sold them, reported them stolen and then claimed on the insurance policy.

There are only so many times you can do that and get away with it.

And then, inevitably perhaps, he was found dead, alone, in his tiny flat.

On the face of it the alcohol had won, as it so often does.

But I know what really killed him.

I dug out a copy of an ancient, dog eared A to Z of Birmingham which I'd used when I'd done some locum work in Birmingham, placed a publicity photograph of him inside it and cremated them together in his memory.

What an unnecessary waste of life.

Childhood

I am always impressed by people who can remember every detail of their childhood. I can't remember all that much of mine.

I remember my Dad building a television around 1949 and waking me up to look at singing and dancing on a small screen on a table in the kitchen. My parents were both very excited and I must have been too because it's my earliest memory.

I can remember discovering that I could read the words in a comic. I was sitting in the back of our car before I'd discovered motion sickness. Suddenly I found that the words meant something.

I remember the coronation of Queen Elizabeth II when every relative who lived within 50 miles arrived to watch the event on our home-made improved television set. It now looked decent because my Dad had also hand crafted a beautifully veneered cabinet. Television sets were rare in those days.

I remember standing upstairs in the spare bedroom watching for the postman to arrive on my birthdays. He used to reach our house at 8.30 am and I had a 30 minute walk to school. If I could see him approaching, I would wait until 8.40 am and then run all the way. I was waiting not for parcels but simply for birthday cards – just to see how many there were. I wouldn't open them until I got home that afternoon but I just wanted to see that there would be some envelopes to open.

I remember Christmas. We had real, live candles on a real, live tree and we had hand-made paper streamers. We also always had a bucket of water next to the tree. Every now and then my Mum would call out 'Ted, the tree's on fire again'. And my Dad would use the bucket of water to put out the fire.

Then we progressed to electric lights which weren't anywhere near as much fun. I can't remember whether the lights were in series or in parallel but whichever it was, it was the variety which meant that when one bulb went the whole lot went out. Dozens of bulbs had to be unscrewed and tested to find the faulty one. The candles and the bucket of water were much easier and far more fun.

I remember the two boys who committed suicide while I was at grammar school. One sat next to me. They both committed suicide because they were struggling with their academic workload and they feared that their families would think them failures. At medical school, a few years later, one of the students with whom I shared a flat gassed himself while we were all out. He had failed an important examination and although he knew he would be allowed to take it again, he obviously feared that he would fail a second time. He was one of the kindest and brightest people I knew. He'd have made a wonderfully sympathetic doctor.

It's not a lot of memories, is it?

But they're as vivid as yesterday.

Maybe more childhood memories will emerge if I get even older.

Kirkby

In the early 1960s, when I was in my final year at school, a man called Alec Dickson came to speak to the sixth form. He was touring the country to promote a new organisation he had founded called Community Service Volunteers. I suppose he must have had some sort of grant to set up the organisation because he wasn't a particularly wealthy man.

Dickson was a retired colonial something or other who was best known for having previously founded Voluntary Service Overseas, the UK version of America's Peace Corps.

He had left VSO (not entirely voluntarily as I recall) and had set up CSV to help young people give a year's voluntary work between leaving school and going on to whatever awaited them in the rest of their lives. The idea, I think, was that the volunteer would help the community into which he was parachuted while, in turn, learning a little about him or herself and about the way other people live. It was the same principle as VSO but without the foreign travel, the expense, the glamour and the thrill of tropical diseases.

Alec Dickson told me I was the first to sign up (and I was certainly the only one from my school) and I have absolutely no idea why I did so.

I was, I suppose, taken by the idea of a small adventure and of putting something back into society before I'd taken anything much out (apart from the beginnings of an education). I've always done things upside down and the wrong way round.

Alec had a commanding manner and within days of my agreeing to give a year of my life to his organisation, he had called me up and sent me to a Cheshire Home in East Grinstead. There I spent two weeks helping out as a general assistant. This mainly consisted of pushing wheelchairs around, feeding people who couldn't feed themselves and wiping other people's bottoms, two activities which had never previously been a part of my life.

The weeks in East Grinstead were, however, merely the hors d'oeuvre. As soon as I got home from there I was sent to Kirkby, just outside Liverpool to be a catalyst. What this meant was that no one had the foggiest idea what I was going to do, how the community was going to react or whether it was going to be a waste of time, a modest disaster or a success.

Technically, I was attached to the local social services department where I was expected to help out with various voluntary organisations, such as the Citizens Advice Bureau and the local Meals on Wheels; and also expected to assist in a youth centre which was called Centre 63 because it was a youth centre and it had been founded in 1963.

Centre 63 was founded by a young priest who later became a bishop and who was considered a very attractive matrimonial prospect by 80% of the single women between the ages of 20 and 85.

Since absolutely no one had ever done anything like this before, I don't think anyone had any more of an idea what to do with me than I knew what to do with them or with myself. It was an experiment, set up by Alec Dickson who had set the wheels in motion and then quietly and sensibly got on with something else.

I had a room in the local vicarage where my breakfast and evening meals were provided, and Community Service Volunteers paid me thirty shillings a week to cover everything else I might need (clothes, bus fares, cinemas, snacks, books, etc.). The vicar with whom I was rooming was a Canon, and every Monday morning I had breakfast with twelve vicars. It was there that I learned to eat my toast with butter or marmalade but never both. I was never sure what this modest self-denial meant in spiritual terms but it's a habit I still have.

I supplemented the modest stipend of thirty bob a week by some modest adventures in the world of freelance journalism. This included writing drama reviews for the local newspaper, the *Kirkby Reporter*. The sum total of my relevant experience for this work was a spell as an Assistant Stage Manager for my school's dramatic society. And, recognising my lack of experience, I was possibly the kindest, most sympathetic and forgiving reviewer there has ever been.

During my time in Kirkby I saw around 150 versions of Oscar Wilde's play *The Importance of Being Earnest*. I should, I suppose, be grateful that the set book for students that year wasn't King Lear. I think 150 versions of King Lear would have finished me off. I knew Wilde's masterpiece by heart at the end and could have easily understudied any of the actors. You would be surprised to know how many different ways there are of directing that play. The only constant was the way that everyone playing the part of Lady Bracknell, made famous by Dame Edith Evans, managed to stretch the words 'A handbag!' into an Act of their own.

I soon found that helping out at the youth club and driving the Meals on Wheels van two or three times a week weren't sufficient to keep me busy, though driving the van was pretty exciting.

The van, probably the least roadworthy vehicle in the North of England, wouldn't have got within a hundred miles of passing an MOT test and smelt forever of cabbage since cabbage played a vital role in the meals I delivered. It was probably that long hidden memory that later led me to write *Mrs Caldicot's Cabbage War*. It's funny how memories hang around out of sight for decades and then peep out without any warning.

Kirkby was like nothing I'd ever known.

I had been brought up in a relatively sensible West Midlands town called Walsall which was famous then for the manufacture of saddles, a division three football team, known locally as The Saddlers, and the annual illuminations in the Arboretum. Oh, and it was almost famous as the birthplace of Jerome K. Jerome, the author of *Three Men in a Boat*, the funniest book ever published. He'd moved away when quite young but Walsall didn't have many literary heroes so we clung to Mr Jerome. There was a statue to him somewhere in the town, though I suspect it's probably been pulled down by now. There was a plaque outside the library too. The library is still there but I don't know about the plaque.

(When I was young Walsall was in Staffordshire but someone moved it as I growing up. These days I get rude letters if I say Walsall is in Staffordshire. But that's where it was when I was a boy and so that's where it will remain as far as my heart is concerned.)

Kirkby in the 1960s had the reputation of being the toughest town in the UK. And many of those living there were curiously proud of this. Just about every shop had a metal grill over its windows and doors at night and most establishments kept the metal grills up during the daytime too. The ones without grills had broken windows and not much stock left. Even the police station was protected with heavy metal grills and several miles of coiled barbed wire. Buses from nearby Liverpool to Kirkby were escorted by police cars and if the escort didn't turn up, the bus didn't move.

I turned up in this inferno wearing my old school uniform because it was pretty much all I'd got to wear – except for my sports coat which I kept for best. When I arrived, the local paper printed a picture of me on the front page. In the picture I am wearing my blazer and my school tie and I look about 12 rather than 18. There was lots of wear left in that blazer, and my old school tie was the only neckwear I had. I wasn't brought up to wear a blazer without a tie.

In retrospect I am amazed I wasn't beaten up as I wandered about the town. I think all that saved me was that I looked completely out of place. No one beat me up because what credit could there possibly be to beating up a kid wearing a school blazer and school tie? No one wore blazers in Kirkby. Pretty well everyone in the town over the age of ten was in a gang, and the gangs didn't know what to make of me. I must have looked like an alien. Anyway, they left me alone. I walked around Kirby, at any time of day or night like the white faced clown in a circus; like Tony Curtis in the Great Race, except that it was half-bricks flying around not custard pies.

Because no one had the faintest idea what I should be doing except driving the Meals on Wheels van and helping out at Centre 63, I decided to start my year by conducting a survey of all the old people in the town. For this I recruited an army of several hundred school-children. We asked everyone over 65 if they needed any decorating or gardening doing. Then, when the survey was finished, we started doing the decorating and attending to the gardens. I couldn't afford to buy paint so I approached a local paint factory. They gave me a van load of the stuff and offered me as much as I needed – all free of charge. I used the Meals on Wheels van to collect the paint, so after a month or so the van smelt of both paint and cabbage.

Things went surprisingly well. There were mishaps, of course. One deaf old lady got her flat painted green when she'd said she'd wanted it cream. But she was so pleased she said she liked green walls and thought they looked rather good. None of my army was molested, attacked, kidnapped or harmed in any way. I like to think they all learnt something. I was enormously proud of them.

The council's trade union bosses quickly complained that we

were doing them out of work that should have been done by their members. I responded by pointing out that the work wasn't being done so there were no losers – only winners. The argument was conducted in the local press. The unions backed down. This all did my credibility no harm at all in a town where authority was a dirty word.

My nearly a year in Kirkby changed me and changed my life as much as anything I've ever done. It turned me into a rebel. It made me question authority. It made me independent. And it gave me the courage to get rid of my blazer.

Just before I left Kirkby, I was interviewed by a reporter from *The Guardian* newspaper. He was curiously complimentary. When I left the town, after about nine months, one of the gangs invited me into their lair above a garage. The leader presented me with a document, signed by them all, which declared me a lifetime member of the gang.

Sadly, the document has long since gone the way of most things but it was one of the most valuable pieces of paper I've ever possessed. I would put it well below my half of our wedding certificate but well above my medical degree, and certainly well above all the other memberships I have acquired, been given or bought in my lifetime.

I've never been back to Kirkby since I left but I do sometimes wonder if the old meals on wheels van is still running.

An Odd Couple

He was the publisher of a stable of magazines which he ran from afar with the aid of enough modern technology to put a rocket into space.

He had moderately raised blood pressure which required a low, maintenance dose of medication and he was, to be polite about it, rather blunt in the way he shared his opinions. Early on in our relationship he explained that he was too rich and too old for subtlety. 'At my age there isn't time for dropping casual hints,' he said.

He wore a Patek Philippe watch which was probably worth as much as a flat in Knightsbridge, and he always made sure that his shirt cuffs were pushed back far enough to ensure that the watch was clearly visible. The first time I met him he managed to introduce the time into the conversation within the first ten minutes, with the topic necessitating a long hard look at his watch. I noticed that he did the same thing with everyone else, even people who were making deliveries. I didn't think the worse of him for this. If you've spent that much on a watch you might as well let people see it.

He had very short legs but quite a longish body and the result was that when he was sitting he looked unusually tall but when he stood he was unusually short. People who only ever met him when he was sitting would have described him as tall and people who met him when he was standing would have described him as short. It was a physical idiosyncrasy which would, I suppose, have been a help if he'd ever been wanted by the police.

She was a retired actress, as round as a balloon. In the early years of her career she had always been type cast as the 'best friend', the 'next door neighbour' or the 'forgotten wife'. Later she had become typecast as 'the secretary who types while the main secretary hands the star a folder' or the 'waitress who walks about in the background while the main waitress serves a meal to the star'.

In her mid-thirties she abandoned her career, which she knew was not going anywhere, divorced her first husband, a gaffer whom she hardly knew since he spent ten months a year away on location, and married the publisher who just happened to be the richest man she'd ever met.

And so she'd moved from Frinton to Paris. I suspect that in terms that matter, that's a far longer distance than it appears to be if you look at a map. She had osteoarthritis in both of her knees, which wasn't surprising considering her weight. I never saw her without absurdly chunky jewellery on her fingers and dangling from her ears. It wasn't costume jewellery. It was always real. She wore a diamond and gold encrusted Rolex watch and she too took great care to ensure that it was always on display. She rarely wore long sleeved blouses or jumpers, and on those occasions when the weather demanded a sweater or a jacket she made sure that the sleeve was rolled up out of the way. She once told me that her personal motto was: 'Whenever I've had enough, I always want more.'

The walls of their apartment were decorated, floor to ceiling, with photographs of her in a wide variety of roles, both on the stage and on film. In much the same way that former army officers will invariably go up a rank when they retire, so all actresses who have appeared in films which have been shown in cinemas (as opposed to being shown exclusively on television) become movie stars when they hang up their false hair extensions.

She'd paid a local print shop to produce some posters of the films she'd been in – with the difference that on her posters her name appeared in prominent type, promoted alongside the names of the stars who had been on the posters when the films had been launched. The posters, expensively framed, hung in the foyer of their apartment.

Although they had been living in Paris for many years, neither of them spoke much French and I think they found the idea of a doctor who was English and who had been trained in England rather comforting. There are many differences between the ways that the English and the French practise medicine. For example, French doctors tend to prescribe a good many of the drugs they use as suppositories. English and American patients can find this rather strange and disturbing. The French find suppositories perfectly normal.

I wasn't practising medicine in France but they used to telephone me regularly to ask for advice about their symptoms and their medication. I never understood why they didn't just find an English or American doctor – there were plenty of them in Paris at the American Hospital.

When we first visited their apartment, she proudly showed us one of their spare bedrooms. It was full of suitcases which I assumed were empty. They weren't. Each suitcase was crammed full of clothes which they had bought on trips to other cities. All the clothes looked to be expensive and all were still in the carrier bags supplied by the shops from which they had been bought. The luggage was all expensive leather – the sort that costs several thousand pounds per case.

'How long have these clothes been in the suitcases?' I asked, astonished.

'Some of them were bought years ago,' she confessed without embarrassment.

(Oddly, I had once known another couple, living in Monaco, who had a similarly stocked room – full of suitcases filled with expensive purchases. The rich seem to gain great satisfaction from just buying and owning. It's a severe form of retail therapy.)

She picked up a beautifully bound, heavy art book from a pile of similar books stacked up on the floor and handed it to me. 'You like books,' she said. 'You'll enjoy this one. We're on page 79.'

I flicked through the pages until I came to page 79. It was a photograph of the two of them sitting, rather self-consciously, on their own sofa. The whole book was full of photographs. I looked at the cover. The title was: 'The 200 Most Important People in Paris'.

I turned the page, and then turned it again. I had not heard of any of the people featured. Most of the pages carried a photograph of one person. A dozen pages had couples on them. One page had three people. The book was incredibly heavy. If you'd screwed four legs onto it, it would have made a great coffee table.

'Did you pay to be in this book?' I asked. It would have been rude if I'd asked the question of anyone else. But it didn't seem rude to ask it of her.

'Oh, no!' she said. 'But the photographer asked us for a cheque for two dozen copies of the book before she took the photograph.'

'And how much did each book cost?'

'I think it was about £150 per book. It's very good quality paper and the photographer is very well known. She's a society photographer. She once took a picture of Prince Rainier.'

I thought for a moment. Twenty four books at £150 per book is £3,600. Multiplied by 200. I could hardly work it out. But eventually I managed it. £720,000.

'Quite a profitable exercise for the photographer,' I said.

'The books are printed on very good expensive paper,' she said.

It seemed a pretty good scam to me.

'How were you chosen to be photographed?' I asked.

'The photographer came to our apartment door and said she'd heard of us. She said she thought we were just the sort of people for her book. In fact she said the book wouldn't be complete without us.'

'Do you know any of the other 199 people in the book?'

She said she didn't.

When we left she insisted we took the book with us. It was so heavy I could hardly carry it.

And when we sold our apartment we left the book behind.

I hope the new owners enjoy it.

Television Days

I have no idea how many TV programmes I've presented or how many times I've appeared on chat shows and discussion shows. Other people always keep lists of all the shows they've done. I once met a professor of something or other who appeared a good deal on television and radio and loved giving lectures and being famous. He had a huge notebook which he carried with him at all times and in which he kept a full record of every programme he'd made. He also kept all his cuttings and carefully pasted them into leather albums which had his initials and the year printed on the cover in gold.

Because of the book promotion tours which I used to do two or three times a year there was a point in the late 1980s when I think I'd been into just about every TV and radio studio in the United Kingdom and Ireland. I toured so much I wrote a guide for *The Bookseller* magazine in which I advised authors on the best car parking places for radio and television studios all over the country.

One year I went to a shindig at Buckingham Palace and I was given a special windscreen sticker so that I could park my car in the courtyard. The sticker, which was huge, said something like 'Buckingham Palace – Courtyard Car Park' and had been glued to my windscreen by a flunky. I kept it there for years because I found it enabled me to park the car more or less wherever I liked. While racing the country on tour I once parked inside a shopping mall because I couldn't find anywhere else to park. When I got back to the car there was a policeman standing beside it. I thought I was in trouble but he saluted and held up the traffic while I backed out onto the road. He had, it seemed, been guarding the car (a rather ancient Volvo) to make sure it wasn't attacked by Republicans. Sadly, I had a crash after two or three years and the windscreen had to be replaced. I did ask the garage to remove and replace my sticker but they couldn't or didn't so that was that. I didn't give a damn about the windscreen but I was gutted about the car park sticker which I remember desperately trying in vain to rescue.

Most of the television shows I made are now just an

indistinguishable blur. Television is the most ephemeral business. You can't even wrap chips in it. And there is so much wasted time. For two years I used to fly up to Scotland once a week to make a BBC programme. I doubt if I ever recorded more than ten or fifteen minutes of television while I was there. The rest of time there I spent writing or reading or replying to mail, usually in my dressing room. The best part about that deal was that every time I got to the studios one of the hairdressers would cut my hair. I didn't have to go to an ordinary hairdresser for two years.

(In those days, there were far fewer rules at airports. One day I wandered bleary eyed onto the tarmac at Birmingham airport, boarded what I thought was my plane and settled down to read through what I was supposed to be doing that day. The doors were locked and a stewardess started explaining how the life-vests worked. I realised something was wrong because the flight from Birmingham to Glasgow doesn't go over the sea. I asked the stewardess where the plane was going. 'Malaga,' she replied. They very kindly stopped the plane, opened the door, brought back the steps and let me out to catch my plane to Glasgow.)

I cannot even remember the name of the programme I was making in Scotland but I do remember that one Christmas I was somehow persuaded to put on a Father Christmas outfit and a pair of what the wardrobe lady insisted where a pair of Robbie Coltrane's Wellington boots and sit between my co-presenters (Barbara Dixon and Penny Junor) on a sofa. As we were waving goodbye (it was a programme which went out in the daytime and presenters did stuff like that in the daytime) I produced a flurry of lingerie from the pockets of my red coat, cried Happy Christmas and sprinkled the items over Barbara and Penny. It wasn't terribly funny but it was unexpected and they both collapsed laughing as the credits rolled. The director thought it was wonderful but he hadn't had his cameras in quite the right place and so we had to do it again. The second time there was no sense of surprise and it was all as flat as a pancake. That, of course, was the take they used.

I can remember two other programmes.

The first was a BBC studio programme involving the South African surgeon Christiaan Barnard who was the first man to perform a heart transplant. I was a medical student at the time and for some long forgotten reason the BBC paid for me to travel to

London to sit in a small audience. They probably also paid me a small fee.

When I arrived at the studios I was, I remember, greeted by the comedian Marty Feldman. He was sitting cross legged on a table in the entrance hall saying 'Welcome to the BBC' to everyone who entered. To every visitor he handed a small bar of chocolate. I don't know whether this was an act of simple generosity or mischief. I have, over the years, found that eating chocolate before talking on the radio or television makes my tongue stick to my teeth and the roof of my mouth. At Lord's Cricket Ground in London, in the 1930s, a kindly old member used to stand at the door to the Long Room and hand a one penny bar of chocolate to every batsman who had been dismissed, and was trudging back through the pavilion on the way to his team's dressing room. A small consolation, I suppose.

For the Barnard programme I sat behind a pundit called Malcolm Muggeridge who was a regular television personality. Floor managers fussed around him constantly. I remember one rushing over, a minute before the programme started, because she had noticed that the laundry mark was visible on the carefully folded handkerchief in the breast pocket of his suit jacket.

My trip to London was a waste of time. I desperately wanted to ask Dr Barnard if he thought anyone would ever perform a brain transplant and if he thought it would be morally justified if they did.

But I couldn't pluck up the courage so I sat on my hands and said nothing. I wish I could remember how the TV people got hold of my name and why on earth they invited me.

The second incident I remember occurred when I was filming on location for one of several TV series that were based on my book *Bodypower*. The location was a mental hospital but I can't remember where it was.

The producer sat me down at a table with three young men I'd never seen before. They were all similarly dressed in jeans and jumpers.

'Two of these men are mental health social workers,' the producer told me. 'The third is a patient with schizophrenia. I want you to talk to them for six minutes and then at the end of that six minutes I want you to decide which one is the schizophrenic.'

I looked at him and then at the three strangers. There were absolutely no give away signs. No one was foaming at the mouth or carrying an axe.

'We're recording it 'as live',' said the producer. 'And whatever happens we'll show that in the programme.'

For some reason, I remember that programme.

I would have felt a complete idiot if I'd got it wrong. (I didn't.)

That's pretty much all I can remember of the best part of a thousand television programmes.

I've wasted a good deal of my life making television and radio programmes which I and everyone else have long since forgotten. I never much liked television. There was just too much boring sitting around for my liking. Still, the feeling was mutual since television didn't like me much either. I was never in the slightest bit photogenic and always thought I was a terrible television performer. I have no idea why anyone ever hired me but the more reluctant I became the bigger the fees I was paid. And, strangely, the bigger the fee that was offered, the more my reluctance faded.

Home Visit

In the distant days when I was a GP, family doctors did a lot of home visits. And inevitably the calls occasionally came at inconvenient moments. Quite a few came through while I was conducting a morning or evening surgery.

Sometimes patients were happy to wait until the surgery had finished. But on other occasions they needed a visit immediately. I always used to ask: 'Do you want me to visit now or can you wait until the surgery has finished?' Simple.

On one occasion, I was called by a patient who thought her husband was having a heart attack. She wanted me to visit immediately. I told the receptionists that I would have to leave the surgery, left apologies for the patients in the waiting room and hurried off to the patient's home.

It was about 5.30 pm and naturally the roads were busy with motorists going home from work. I turned on my headlights and hazard flashers so that people could see me coming and drove as fast as I could. I was, I remember, driving a bright orange Saab 99 at the time. It was a turbo model with a fine turn of speed.

I can't remember what was wrong with him (probably a bad attack of indigestion) but the patient wasn't having a heart attack.

I stayed a few minutes, soothed him and his wife, prescribed whatever was appropriate and drove back to the consulting rooms to finish the evening surgery.

I didn't think any more of it until a day or so later when I received a telephone call from the secretary to a local Chief Superintendent who was something significant at the local police station. His secretary wanted me to go along to the local police station. Apparently, the policeman, who was a specialist in traffic offences, had been in one of the cars I had passed while driving to my patient. He had tried to catch me but had failed and, as an alternative, he had taken my car number and traced my name and address.

I didn't see why I should go along to the police station so I didn't go.

And a few days later I received a summons for driving with my hazard flashers on.

I had to go to court and the Medical Defence Union sent a high powered lawyer up from London to defend me.

In the end I was fined £5 for driving with my hazards flashers switched on. That was it. My driving licence remained unblemished. I was told that only bus drivers can drive with their flashers going and only then when they have been hijacked and need to attract the attention of the constabulary.

The story hit most of the national newspapers, and one reporter asked me why I thought the policeman wanted me to go along to the police station.

I said I assumed that he wanted to tell me off. Even now, it seemed a logical thought. I can't imagine that he would have suddenly succumbed to a yearning to invite me for tea and biscuits.

And at this point things got very silly.

One of the papers reported that I had said that the policeman had wanted to browbeat me into making an apology.

I had never said any such thing but that, apparently, was no defence when the Chief Superintendent sued me for libel.

Oh dear.

A very eminent barrister in London said he would have loved to have cross-examined the policeman in the witness box but sensibly suggested that the case really wasn't worth the effort. I ended up paying £200 in damages for the comment I hadn't made, and agreeing to the printing of a small apology in the local newspaper. Heaven knows what the legal costs came to. Mine were paid by the Medical Defence Union and the policeman's were, I think, paid by some sort of police body.

McBain

Lawrence Block, who writes excellent thrillers, produced a book about his favourite crime writers. There is a chapter about Evan Hunter (aka Ed McBain and a host of other names).

Here is one paragraph that sums up Mr McBain: 'In his mid-seventies, after a couple of heart attacks, an aneurysm, and a siege of cancer that had led to the removal of his larynx, Evan did something that sums up the man. He decided that what the reading public most wanted was books about women in jeopardy, so he sat down and, as Ed McBain, wrote a book called *Alice in Jeopardy*. And went to work right away on *Becca in Jeopardy*, with every intention of working his way through the alphabet.'

'Don't you love it? Here's a man with one foot in the grave and the other on a banana peel, and he's perfectly comfortable launching a twenty six book series.'

McBain and Hunter (the same man, of course) wrote a remarkable book about their cancer and other illnesses (called *Let's Talk*) and I read it recently. It is awe inspiring. Even while having treatment, and spending weeks in hospital, McBain (even that wasn't his real name which was Salvatore Albert Lombino – I can't imagine why he changed it) produced more new books than most writers do in a decade. And they were all excellent books.

I nearly met Mr Hunter/McBain once.

We were both booked to speak at a Birmingham Post Literary Dinner and for reasons which I can't remember I couldn't go. I'd just finished a three week promotional tour for my book *Mindpower* and I was knackered – certainly too tired to trek all the way to Birmingham to speak at a literary dinner and sell half a dozen books.

It's something I've regretted ever since. He was a beautiful writer and it would have been a privilege to meet him.

Another regret to add to the pile that seems to grow every day.

Jimmy

For reasons long forgotten, I decided to spend a couple of months working in Switzerland.

I'd just finished the best part of a year in Liverpool as a Community Service Volunteer and my next port of call was Birmingham Medical School.

With the help of a man who was a friend of my father's (nepotism but in a very mild way) I got a job as a draughtsman in a factory which was situated in a beautiful little town called Schaffhausen, the most famous part of which is an absolutely magnificent waterfall called the Rheinfalls.

Since Schaffhausen was a German speaking part of Switzerland, I thought it would be a good way to learn German.

Unfortunately, I hadn't realised that the Swiss speak a unique form of German called Schweizerdeutsch. Whenever I tried to use my German in later life people thought I was Swiss.

I was 18-years-old. I got off the train, found a small, cheap hotel and wandered into a café to find something to eat. The café was tiny but to my surprise there was a band playing. There was no stage and they, or someone, had pushed back a third of the tables and chairs to make room for the band and their instruments. To my even greater surprise there was a sign standing on the floor stating that the band's name was Jimmy and the Rackets and that they were from Liverpool.

I ate and listened and since I'd just come from Liverpool, I went up and spoke to the band when they were having a break. (In those days I had far more courage than I could possibly find today.)

It turned out that they weren't from Liverpool at all.

'We say that because of the Beatles and the other Liverpool bands,' said Jimmy (whose name really was Jimmy – Jimmy Duncombe). It turned out that the band had previously been called The Purple Hearts. They'd acquired that name because they'd been playing in a bar in Germany, at a US Army Base, when there'd been some fighting.

'We carried on playing while the chairs were flying around,' said the drummer. 'So they called us The Purple Hearts. And that stuck.'

I have no idea why they changed their name again. Bands used to do that a good deal as they struggled for success.

The odd thing was that Jimmy and the Rackets had been massively successful in Germany. They'd had a string of number one hit records.

I asked them if they'd mind if I wrote a story about them for the *Liverpool Echo*.

'But we're not from Liverpool,' protested one of them.

'I know,' I said. 'That's the story. Do you mind?'

They said they didn't mind at all.

So I wrote the story out in longhand, pointing out that Liverpool was now so famous as the world centre of music that bands which had never been there described themselves as 'From Liverpool'. I then stuffed the article in an envelope, bought a stamp and posted it to the *Echo*. They duly used it and sent me a cheque.

The other day I looked up Jimmy and the Rackets on the internet. And then I bought a CD of them playing. I have to admit that they weren't the greatest band in the world. But I remember they made a hell of a fine noise in that small café.

Journalism

I cannot remember ever not having a notebook and pencil in my pocket. When I was at school I was writing short articles and stories for magazines. I even tried my hand at cartoons and managed to sell quite a few.

Things became a bit more serious when I went to Liverpool as a Community Service Volunteer. I knew absolutely no one, I was living in a vicarage (which had no television) and although I knew my days would be busy, I also knew I'd need to find something to do in the evenings, other than sit and read all the books I'd crammed into my suitcase.

I bought myself a Teach Yourself Typewriting book and a very old, sit up and beg typewriter with sticky keys and a distorted letter 'e'. The machine had been built in the 19th century and in order to insert a capital letter it was necessary to press a lever which lifted half the typewriter up into the air. The machine had a carriage return which had a tendency to shoot off to the right and land on the floor. The keys were bent and tended to stick together for companionship. There were no ribbons available for it so I had to buy ribbons which fitted newer machines and wind them onto the elderly metal spools. I seemed to remember that the machine cost £5 and weighed around a ton and a quarter.

I did enrol for a typing course and short hand class at the local technical college but I was the only male in the class and the college principal asked me to leave after one class. She said the class was for girls and she thought there was a risk I might turn out to be a disruptive influence. So, I carried on with my Teach Yourself book and became a speedy typist, though my sticking keys did sometimes mean that the pages I typed looked as though they were written in Polish. I acquired a habit of hammering the keys rather hard, and as a result, I still tend to destroy keyboards at an unusual rate.

I know mechanical typewriters are old-fashioned but I do miss mine. It had quirks, foibles and eccentricities but it never once chose to turn a page of text red or to convert everything to italics. (I find that modern word processing programmes are counter-intuitive and enormously irritating.) I've had a number of typewriters over the years (my favourite old Olympia still sits in its case, ready for the day when there is no electricity available) but that one has a big place in the small corner of my heart reserved for machinery.

Gathering up all the courage of youth I wandered into the office of the local newspaper, *The Kirkby Reporter*, and asked if they had any work I could do. I was wearing my dear old school blazer and tie, grey flannels and sensible school shoes. I only had one other jacket (a sports coat which I kept for Sundays) and one other pair of shoes (ditto).

The editor, shirt sleeved, tousled, and lost in a cloud of cigarette smoke, asked what I was doing there and who I was. I explained. Someone took a photograph, the editor wrote some words and they put me on that week's front page. It was probably a slow week and they were fed up with having burning buses and smashed shop window on the front page.

'Can you review plays?' the editor asked, when he'd written his 'splash'.

I said I thought I could.

It turned out that the paper received a constant stream of invitations to attend local productions and that, since no one from the paper was interested, no one ever went. There were a few professional productions in and around Liverpool but most of the invitations were to school productions. I became the paper's drama critic and they paid me 30 shillings for each review. They also paid my bus fares. I learned to scribble notes in the dark. I bought a pen which lit up a little when you wrote with it but I was too embarrassed to use it. I typed out my reviews on my sit up and beg machine and took them into the newspaper office like a proper journalist.

I learned a lot from *The Kirkby Reporter*.

I remember being in there one press day when they had nothing to put on the front page: absolutely nothing. The newspaper office was on the first floor above a shop in a shopping precinct and there was a bookie's shop directly opposite.

'I've been watching the people going into the bookies,' said the editor suddenly. He put a piece of paper into his typewriter, which wasn't a lot younger than mine. 'Two thirds of them are women.' He sent the photographer down to take a picture of the front of the bookies and a young reporter down to talk to a couple of the customers.

Thirty minutes later he had his front page story. It was all about housewives putting the grocery money on a horse in the 3.30 at Exeter. It was a great story. There was a great headline too. 'Gambling Fever in Kirkby'. He gave the story some strength with a quote from a friendly, local social worker and a quote from a contact at the police station. There were links to drugs and alcoholism.

True, it was a manufactured story; created in 30 minutes out of nothing. But it was relevant and it was significant and it drew attention to a genuine problem.

It was an entire journalism course in half an hour.

I spent nine months in Liverpool and three months working in a factory in Switzerland. I then went to medical school, knowing a hell of a lot more about the world than if I'd gone straight there from school.

As soon as I arrived in Birmingham, I walked into the offices of the *Birmingham Post* newspaper and asked if they needed someone to review plays. I had my little folder of cuttings from the *Kirkby Reporter* and copies of scores of articles I'd written for magazines.

An Assistant Editor, a lovely, kind man called Leslie Duckworth, who also wrote books on cricket, kindly pointed out to me that they already had two professional drama critics, JC Trewin and Michael Billington, but they could use me as a third string.

'Would I review amateur productions and school plays?' he asked.

Of course I would. I'd review anything.

And Mr Duckworth introduced me to Keith Brace, the literary editor, who wondered if I'd review books for the paper.

Of course I would. I'd read a lot of books. I knew about books. But as I had been with plays, in my early days as a drama critic, I was endlessly forgiving and uncommonly generous in my reviewing. I was painfully aware of the extent of my ignorance.

Mr Brace (never Keith) used to work out what I'd earned and then pay me in books to the value of the cheque I should have been given. This was fine enough, and quickly gave me a huge library, but I'd have rather had the money.

The best perk was that the paper had an account with a taxi

company – which was a definite step up from catching buses. When reviewing plays I could use their taxi service free of charge instead of standing at bus-stops waiting for buses that never came. And Mr Duckworth said *The Birmingham Post* would pay me £3 for each review. Gold, indeed.

Since my reviews had to be written within minutes of the end of the performance, I learned to write quickly and to dictate my copy to a copy taker. This meant finding a working telephone. Since plays often didn't finish until 10.30 pm and my copy needed to be in before 11.00 pm in order to get into the next morning's edition, I had to move quickly. I usually managed to identify the nearest telephone before a play started and then made a beeline for it before other playgoers occupied the box to call for a taxi or a relative to fetch them. Sometimes, if I was reviewing at a school, I had to walk a mile to find a working phone box. Occasionally, if the play was performed at a venue close to the *Birmingham Post's* offices close to the city centre, I would wander into the news room. The news editor would find me a desk and a typewriter and when I'd finished I'd hand the pages to a copy boy.

It was just like the movies.

The Policeman's Wife

She sat down, crossed her legs demurely and kept her handbag clutched firmly on her lap. She looked around the surgery and then at me. I smiled encouragingly and tried not to say 'How can I help you?' or 'What can I do for you?' I said those things when I began but quickly realised that either made me sound like an assistant in a department store.

'It's very embarrassing,' she said, at last.

'That's alright,' I said, reassuringly. 'You can tell me. That's what I'm here for.'

'I wet myself,' she said suddenly and then blushed.

'How often does it happen?'

'All the time. I don't seem able to hold it in.'

'Does coughing or laughing make it worse?'

'Not particularly,' she said. 'I have to wear two pairs of underwear and a pad.'

I asked if there were any other symptoms. She said there were none.

'And there is something else I want to talk to you about,' she said.

'What's that?'

'We've been trying for a baby for two years,' she said. 'But we don't seem to get anywhere.'

'How often...?'

'Twice a week,' she said. 'Wednesdays and Sundays. My husband is a policeman. I think you know him.'

I glanced at the name on her medical records envelope. I suddenly realised who her husband was. He'd nearly arrested me a month earlier for parking on double yellow lines outside the chemist's. He'd been quite nice about it though and had let me off with a warning.

'Well, let's try to deal with the incontinence first,' I suggested. 'Pop behind the screen, slip your dress off and climb up on the couch.' My consulting room was very small. There wasn't really room for a screen but I thought it added a touch of professionalism.

My predecessor hadn't bothered with one.

A minute later I had solved both problems.

Her husband, the policeman, had been depositing his semen in her urethra rather than her vagina.

'Oh,' she said, 'how silly of us.' She blushed again. 'I did think it was very tight to start with, and it did hurt a lot, but I was a virgin when we married and I thought it was just normal.'

I told her not to worry and lied and assured her that it was a mistake a lot of people made.

Ten months later she had a baby.

And the incontinence was improving.

Vadim

A few decades ago, when the BBC was still a broadcaster and hadn't become a propaganda unit, I used to appear on a programme called 'Start the Week' from time to time – invariably because I had a new book coming out.

One week, I remember being in the studio at Broadcasting House watching the clock tick round to nine o'clock. I was quite young – thirty something I suspect, which seems quite young now – but I can't remember what book I was trying to sell.

A newsreader called Richard Baker was the host and the other guests included David Attenborough and a clump of television celebrities. I can't remember who else was there. We were sitting around a round table, most of us looking early morning dishevelled, and the chair next to me was unoccupied.

'It looks as though our other guest isn't coming,' said Richard Baker, as the minute hand on the studio clock showed that the time was nine o'clock. We could hear a news announcer reading the top of the hour news. 'The film director Roger Vadim was due to be our other guest,' said Baker.

I'd heard of Vadim, of course. He was famous for some of the films he'd made but also for the women in his life. By the time he'd finished he'd had well recorded romances with Brigitte Bardot , Catherine Deneuve and Jane Fonda. He may have married some or all of them.

Suddenly, as we all cleared our throats and the news reader started to wind up, the outer door to the studio was flung open. We all turned and there was Roger Vadim – immaculately dressed and with a beautiful overcoat slung over his shoulders in a French superstar sort of way.

Either side of him stood a statuesque blonde – they looked as though they'd been hired straight from Central Casting. They too were immaculate and looked as though they were ready for dinner at the Ritz.

The clock ticked away.

With a few seconds to go, the two women each plucked a shoulder of Vadim's coat and lifted it from him. Vadim, freed of the encumbrance, stepped into the outer room where the sound engineer sat, opened the door to the studio and slid effortlessly into the empty chair. He said good morning to me, since I was next to him, on his left, nodded to everyone else, and Richard Baker said good morning to the audience.

It was the most impressive entrance I have ever seen. And it was all for a radio programme. The only audience members who saw this amazing performance were those of us around the table and the engineer in the outer room.

I realised then, more than ever, that there are other worlds I would never fully understand. The idea of making all that effort to impress five or six strangers just seemed bizarre.

Mountaineer

I often buy old magazines and newspapers and find that they are invariably full of surprising nuggets of information and entertainment.

Really old newspapers are infinitely more fun than new ones because nothing in them matters; everything has been sanitised by the passage of time. And old magazines often contain quite extraordinary accounts of adventure.

For example, I recently read an article entitled 'Albert Smith's Ascent of Mont Blanc' which appeared in *Blackwood's Magazine* in January 1852. As always with such articles the preparation for the trip are almost as fascinating as the adventure itself. Smith, who was, I discovered, a doctor who had become a professional writer, was climbing with a couple of chums and a pair of guides. Naturally, they climbed in tweed jackets, tweed trousers and stout boots. But it was the provisions Smith and his companions took with them for the climb (and for the two nights which they spent on the mountain) which really astonished me.

Here is the list Smith included in his article:

60 bottles of vin ordinaire
6 bottles of Bordeaux
10 bottles of St George
15 bottles of St Jean
3 bottles of Cognac
1 bottle of Syrup of raspberries
6 bottles of Lemonade
2 bottles of Champagne
20 loaves
10 small cheeses
6 Packets of chocolate
6 Packets of sugar
4 Packets of prunes
4 Packets of raisins
2 packets of salt

4 Wax candles
6 Lemons
4 legs of mutton
4 shoulders of mutton
6 pieces of veal
1 piece of beef
11 large fowls
35 small fowls

The Hat Dance

As we walked around Paris one spring day, Antoinette suddenly decided that the hat she was wearing was too tight. It had, she said, been a little tight when we had started our walk but it had become tighter by the minute. She asked me to help her stretch it. So she removed the hat, she took one side and I took the other and we both pulled as hard as we could. Within a minute we had gathered quite a crowd of interested spectators. Not wanting to let them down, and feeling that we owed it to the area to provide some sort of spectacle, I suddenly let go of my side of the hat and shouted 'All right, you can have the bloody hat!'

Antoinette, caught on immediately, looked pleased with her 'victory' and put the hat back on her head. The crowd dispersed, doubtless pleased with the outcome.

Impromptu street theatre.

It only occurred to me later that we should have collected money. We might have done quite well. If times get hard we'll work it up into a bit of a routine.

Napoleon

When I was a medical student we didn't have long summer holidays (as other students did) and so there wasn't much opportunity for travel or to find a job for a few weeks. This always seemed to me rather a pity because it kept medical students away from real life experience.

There was one exception: in the summer following our first year's studies, we did have a couple of months off from work.

During that last summer of freedom, a chum and I decided that we would buy cheap train tickets and go to Italy. My chum was feeling glum because he and his girlfriend had just parted company. He had bought a 1926 Bugatti 35A racing car for next to nothing and used it to drive around Birmingham. Like all racing cars it made a good deal of noise. He swapped the Bugatti for an ancient Jeep when his girlfriend complained that sitting with her legs astride the tail of the racing car was uncomfortable and dangerous, especially when they'd been to the pub. She had managed to burn herself several times on the exhaust pipe. Sadly, she also complained about the Jeep, which had no roof or windows and the relationship was over by the time we went abroad. (It was a pity that he got rid of the Bugatti which was unusual and would now be worth a considerable fortune.)

Our trip was, to say the least, an educational experience. We took a small tent (so small that we both had to sleep with our feet outside, exposed to the elements) and a tiny and rather explosive stove upon which we could prepare delicacies such as baked beans and, well, more baked beans.

We very nearly drowned in the sea just off Pisa where we got caught in a riptide and had to swim about half a mile along the coast to find a spot where we were able to reach the shore. We both waved and shouted help but people on the beach just waved back merrily.

But the highlight of the trip was a visit to the island of Elba where we pitched our tent on a sandy beach, just above the high water line. We did very little while we were there, though I did grow a moustache; one of those hairy Zapata style moustaches that made me look like a 'before' picture for an advertisement for razor blades. It also resulted in my looking nothing like my passport photo, with the inevitable result that our travels through custom posts were made rather more time consuming and hazardous than they might otherwise have been.

Elba is, of course, well known as the temporary home of Napoleon in 1814 after he was thrown out of France, and so while we were there we visited the small museum commemorating his residence. There were the usual souvenirs for sale, including countless pictures and models of Napoleon on a horse, Napoleon on foot and Napoleon in bust form only. Today there are probably Napoleon candles and little models of Napoleon in plastic domes filled with water and fake snow.

I didn't buy any of the gewgaws but I did purchase a photocopy of a small leaflet which Napoleon had ordered to be printed when he planned his escape from the island and his long journey back to Paris to reclaim the throne he had long regarded as his by right.

The leaflet, or flyer, was printed on one side only and was headed 'L'Empereur Napoleon: A l'Armee.' The next line was simply Soldats.

Compiled in 1815, it was without a doubt the most brilliant political leaflet every written. It was almost certainly written by Napoleon himself.

The first few words are: 'We have not been beaten…'

Napoleon knew that the authorities had learned that he was planning to escape and head up through Italy and France back to the French capital. And he knew that the French army had been sent to stop him, arrest him and return him to the island. If Napoleon resisted, and returning him wasn't possible, the order was to kill him.

Napoleon (who knew all about publicity as well as marketing) left the island Elba riding his white horse. He had with him the loyal guards who had, supposedly, been guarding him.

Going north, and heading for Paris, the exiled Emperor met the French army heading south.

This was the moment of truth and it should have been the end of Napoleon. If it had been the end of him the Peninsular War wouldn't have happened, the future Duke of Wellington would have remained an unknown soldier, there would have been no Battle of Waterloo and European history would have been very different.

But Napoleon had enough self-confidence for a whole platoon of reality TV stars and as the arresting party approached he rode forward, alone, while he companions rode to the flanks and distributed copies of his leaflets to the soldiers who might not be able to hear what their Emperor was saying. It was, perhaps, the first mass mailing in history. It was certainly the most successful.

Almost instantly the soldiers of the French army (sent, remember, to arrest or kill him) turned their horses and fell in behind their beloved General. Napoleon was back.

Napoleon then led his army back to Paris and reappointed himself Emperor.

Not surprisingly, the next time Napoleon was arrested (after his defeat at Waterloo) he was sent a little further away – to St Helena.

Many years later I managed to purchase at auction a collection of original handwritten documents signed by Napoleon during his island residence. I paid considerably more for these than I had for the photocopy of Napoleon's glorious leaflet.

But the leaflet affected me far more, as is illustrated by the fact that today I was able to lay my hands on it within moments but it took me ages to find where I'd put the valuable, handwritten documents.

Trivia in Medicine

The other day, I heard an eminent doctor talking on the wireless about medical problems.

I don't remember much that he said (he was very boring and long-winded) but I do remember that he stated, quite categorically, that doctors should not waste their valuable time on trivial medical problems. He was, as you might imagine, a doctor who had probably never syringed an ear or taken a blood pressure. He was one of those doctors who earn a very good living sitting on committees and boards and acting as a consultant and advisor to a wide variety of different commercial groups and drug companies.

His argument was that the sort of problems which he described as trivial should be dealt with by nurses, auxiliaries or even clerical assistants.

He was talking bollocks.

I haven't practised medicine for a good while but I did practise for ten years, I paid attention and I can remember what it was like. I can also remember that general practice in England then was, from the patient's point of view, a great deal better in every way than it is now, or is ever likely to be in the future.

Far too many people in the medical establishment spend their days running round in circles, never looking where they were going, but always pretending to be making progress. It is a crying shame that all the really important decisions in medicine are made by administrators, bureaucrats and politicians – people who have absolutely no day to day practical experience of what patients need, or how they are best diagnosed and treated.

When I heard that eminent practitioner, stalwart of the medical establishment, pontificating about the insignificance of medical problems which he sniffily dismissed as 'trivial', I almost threw my coffee cup at the wireless. It is a good job that I hadn't been driving at the time.

I disagreed violently with the old fool for several reasons; but mainly because I believe that it was a very dangerous attitude.

The truth is that there are no really trivial problems in medicine. Seemingly quite small health problems may mean a great deal to a patient. Problems which a doctor might recognise as relatively insignificant may be a real worry to a patient. Problems which might appear to be trivial may be hiding a really important health problem. Minor symptoms, dismissed as trivial, might herald the early development of diabetes, cancer or heart disease.

Is it trivial when someone has a lipoma on their skin? It's benign and easy to remove but it might make the patient's life unbearable. A schoolteacher with a lipoma on the top of his head might be ragged mercilessly by his pupils. He might want to give up work because of this 'trivial' condition. What about if a man has gynaecomastia? Is that trivial? It might seem so to the observer. Someone with wax in their ears might think that they are going deaf. Is that trivial?

In addition, I believe that by personally attending to relatively simple medical tasks, things which perhaps could be handed over to a nurse, the doctor is able to build his relationship with his patients. This is important because in due course the strength of that relationship might prove vital if the patient acquires a serious or life threatening disorder. Within seconds of switching off the wireless in disgust I was able, without much thought, to come up with a couple of incidents which prove my point that it is foolish for doctors to hand any health problems over to nurses or auxiliaries.

So, for example, there was Mr Oliver Padgett.

Mr Padgett came into the surgery complaining of indigestion. 'I wonder if you could give me something stronger than the stuff I can buy at the chemist?' he asked.

Now, indigestion is almost certainly one of those health problems which the eminent practitioner would be inclined to dismiss as 'trivial' – easily within the remit of an assistant who could simply arrange for a prescription to be written out. But is it always so easily dismissed?

I asked Mr Padgett, who was in his forties and rather overweight, how long he had indigestion.

'Oh, a few months,' he told me. And he proceeded to give a perfect medical history of a man with indigestion. His pain only came on after he had eaten. It seemed to go away if he swallowed a little antacid. And so on and so forth.

I was tempted to succumb and write out a prescription for

something to ease his indigestion pain.

But it was only after I had talked to him that I began to suspect that things might not be quite as simple as they appeared to be.

'Do you get any other symptoms?' I asked him.

'I get a bit breathless,' he said. 'But I put that down to wind in my stomach.'

'Anything else?'

'A bit sweaty occasionally. But the pain is pretty bad sometimes so it's not surprising that it makes me sweat.'

'Whereabouts is the pain?'

'Across my chest,' he replied, without hesitation.

And at this point the warning bells began to ring because the pain of indigestion is usually much more specific. Indeed, patients sometimes point to their stomach with one finger to show just where they feel the pain.

'Does the pain go anywhere else?'

'I get a pain in my arm sometimes.'

And now the alarm bells were ringing so loudly that they were probably audible in the next county.

'Do you only ever get the pain when you eat?'

'Well, actually, I get it several times a day. It does come on sometimes when I'm eating.'

'But sometimes when you're not eating?'

He nodded.

'And the antacid medicine helps the pain?'

'Sometimes, it does. A little.'

'Do you do anything else to ease the pain?'

'I sit down and take things easy for a while.'

'And then the pain goes?'

'Oh yes.'

'But it could be sitting down and resting that helps get rid of the pain?'

'I suppose it could.'

And, indeed, so it proved to be.

Mr Padgett was getting angina and heart pain. His problem was anything but trivial.

If he had simply been given a bottle of antacid and sent on his way he would have probably had a huge heart attack and died.

Miss Kenshaw was another patient the eminent doctor (the one who doesn't have time for trivial problems) would have preferred to pass onto an aide or some kind.

Miss Kenshaw, a maiden lady in her 50s, came to my surgery complaining that she could no longer hear very well.

'I work as a telephonist,' she told me. 'Having good hearing is vital.'

She was clearly worried about losing her job. It was clear that her work was terribly important to her.

A peep into her ears showed that both of them were pretty well blocked with wax. I got out the brass tray and the large brass syringe which I used to syringe wax out of ears and I managed to remove an enormous quantity of the stuff from her external auditory canals. To be honest, I was surprised that Miss Kenshaw had been able to hear anything at all.

A lot of doctors tell their practice nurse to do the ear syringing. They consider such simple work to be beneath them. But I've always preferred to do these things myself. A doctor can build up a good relationship with a patient by helping him or her to hear again. It's one of those simple jobs which produces a large dividend in terms of goodwill.

However, when I'd finished clearing out Miss Kenshaw's ears I could tell that there was something else still worrying her. I sat her down and told her I wanted her to wait a while before leaving the surgery. This was, in any case, a good idea. Patients can sometimes feel a little dizzy after they've had warm water squirted into their ears. And while she was sat there I asked her if there was anything else she wanted to talk to me about.

I was hoping that she tell me what I sometimes think of the 'sting'.

(The sting always comes at the end of a consultation. After discussing some relatively minor problem, something which eminent practitioners would dismiss as trivial', nervous patients will often say 'by the way' or more commonly 'while I am here' and then introduce the problem they've really been worrying about all along. This second problem will invariably be something complex which will involve a full medical examination and a good deal of brain work. The doctor, who thought he was ready to go on to the next patient, will find himself starting the consultation all over again. This sort of thing often happens because the patient is nervous and too frightened or embarrassed to discuss their 'big' worry. The 'trivial' problem is introduced as a 'foot in the door', an opening gambit, designed to 'warm' up the relationship between doctor and patient. Of course, doctors can sometimes apply their own version of the 'sting'. They wait until the patient is actually touching the door handle and then say something like 'And, of course, no alcohol for six months' or 'Naturally, you mustn't resume normal sexual relations until I see you again. Come and see me in three months.')

At first, Miss Kenshaw denied that she was worried about anything else. But I'd been a GP long enough to know that there was something she wasn't telling me. Family doctors need to be as good at doing this as parents are at squeezing the truth out of their children.

And, sure enough, Miss Kenshaw eventually told me her feared secret which, I am pleased to say I was able to deal with successfully. (She thought she had bowel cancer because she had passed a little blood. In fact she had piles.)

I honestly doubt if any of that would have come to light if Miss Kenshaw had merely come to the surgery, seen a nurse and had her ears syringed in a routine sort of way.

Idiomatic English in France

When we lived in Paris, I found that the French loved nothing better than correcting a foreigner's pronunciation.

And so I liked to get my own back by teaching English idioms to those Parisians who thought they spoke perfect English.

I liked to introduce them to idiomatic phrases such as 'Tally ho!', 'Right ho old boy!'. 'Odds bodkins' and 'What ho!'

It tickled me to hear them dropping these phrases into their daily conversation.

I particularly liked to teach them to use the Shakespearean phrase 'the game's afoot'. (P.G.Wodehouse once bumped into Conan Doyle in New York. Doyle was hunting down publishers who had printed pirated editions of his Sherlock Holmes stories. Wodehouse was tickled pink when Doyle announced that 'the game's afoot!')

Other favourite phrases for sharing with the French included 'Hither and yon', 'Pip pip', and 'My dear old thing'. I taught them to use the saying 'Close of Play' (an English phrase derived from the cricket field) to indicate the end of the working day.

'May I crave a boon?' I might say to the Frenchman who thought he spoke excellent English. He would probably appear puzzled. I'd then explain that it was a very common English phrase that he should add to his repertoire.

In my experience, all French people think they speak excellent English. Even when they are unintelligible they think they speak excellent English. I always praised them all. 'English is a very tricky language,' I would say kindly. 'Foreigners always have difficulty in mastering it. But you're doing quite well. You should persevere. Add some idioms to your vocabulary and you will soon reach a point where English people will be able to understand you without too much difficulty.')

Few things sound funnier than an earnest Frenchman saying 'He cocked a snook!', 'What a fine kettle of fish' or 'The game's afoot, eh?'.

It was important, I found, to teach them to introduce the idioms into ordinary conversation.

I also found it fun to create slightly bastardised idioms.

Here are some I created for distributing among the snootiest Parisians of my acquaintance: 'He dug himself into a corner'; 'Never punch a gift horse in the mouth'; 'He was as healthy as a harp'; 'It was like looking for a milkmaid in haystack'; 'Never steal someone's lightning'; 'Give someone the cold elbow' and 'He punched the bucket'.

If you hear a Frenchman come out with one of these phrases I'd like the credit to be all mine.

You might wonder what it has to do with the price of fish but it's a legacy of which I'm proud.

Fear

Fear is a strange thing. We build it up or push it out of our minds for all sorts of curious reasons. Here's a quote from Tazio Nuvolari, the Italian racing driver, who knew a little more than most about fear and how to put it into perspective.

Nuvolari had just been asked how he found the courage to climb into a racing car when he knew how many other drivers had died.

'Tell me, do you think you will die in bed?' asked Nuvolari. 'You do? Then, where do you find the courage to get into it every night?'

Touring

During the 1970s, 1980s and 1990s I toured Britain at least twice a year, visiting national and local television and radio stations as well as meeting journalists from newspapers and magazines. These promotional tours were always designed to sell a new book (sometimes a hardback edition and sometimes a paperback version) and they were hard work. More than once I got lost and couldn't remember where I was heading or why. (I wasn't the first to have this problem. G.K.Chesterton is reported to have arrived in a town in the Midlands and then sent a telegram to his wife saying: 'Am in Wolverhampton. Why?)

The dangers were endless.

I once visited Yorkshire to promote a health book and, during an interview with a newspaper journalist, I got cramp in my leg because the chairs in which we were sitting were too small and uncomfortable. When we stood up to leave I rubbed my leg to ease the cramp. The journalist devoted the greater part of her article to my temporary affliction – using this bit of nonsense to claim that I clearly wasn't fit enough to be writing on health matters.

And sometimes the results were merely comical. I several times toured under other names, foolishly thinking no one would recognise me. I was once interviewed by a TV station in Birmingham when the interviewer began by saying: 'Vernon, why are you calling yourself Edward Vernon and why have you grown a beard?'

Occasionally, I'd be accompanied by a publicity girl (they were always girls and never boys in those days) who wanted to meet the presenters, editors and producers they spoke to on the telephone but had probably never met, but mostly I'd either go by train or drive myself. It was always difficult to know which was the least stressful. I usually had to hit at least three or four interviews per day.

However long the tour, I used to travel with just a fishing bag which I could carry on one shoulder. The publicity people didn't always travel so lightly. I'll never forget a trip to Belfast and Dublin which I made accompanied by a public relations person who travelled with two huge and very heavy suitcases. I remember struggling into the BBC in Belfast and having to fight to get through the bomb proof doors with her suitcases. I was breathless and exhausted by the time of the interview.

Most of the interviewers I met were courteous and thoughtful and although they had hardly ever read the book I was promoting, they were always well aware that our relationship was symbiotic rather than parasitic.

Occasionally, however, I would come across a pompous fool. These usually worked for BBC local radio and considered themselves very important indeed.

Two stick out for the awfulness.

First, in the 1970s I wrote a book called *Thomas Winsden's Cricketing Almanack* which was a spoof of Wisden, the cricket annual. The book was called *Winsden's Cricketing Almanack* and it was supposedly written by a certain Thomas Winsden. It was, of course, a spoof on *Wisden* – the real cricket almanac – and everywhere I went I had to put up with humourless sports reporters telling me that the publishers had spelt the name of the book wrongly. The book was full of silly biographies, facts and figures and lists of teams made up of fictional players (with Long John Silver being a specialist short leg fielder). I remember that instead of a table of batting averages I had a table of sandwich makers – listing, for example, the women who had most cucumber or cheese and pickle sandwiches for club teas. Some people loved it (David Shepherd, a test match umpire, told me that for some time he had a copy in the pocket of his white coat) and some people didn't understand it at all (the *Daily Telegraph* rang the publisher to ask if he knew that there was a misprint on the cover and throughout the book because the name *Wisden* had been spelt wrongly) and some people simply didn't approve of it.

I did do a lot of interviews for that book.

Nick Owen, a huge cricket fan, interviewed me at TV AM and loved it, and in Yorkshire I was interviewed by Richard Whiteley who was a good chum whom I met often because he presented a local TV news programme. (Dickie Bird was in the studio at the same time and when he saw I was wearing an MCC tie he shied away from me very nervously. A couple of days earlier he and another umpire had been jostled and shouted at when they wouldn't resume play in a Test Match at Lords.)

A well-known cricket commentator at one radio station was so incensed that anyone should write a spoof of *Wisden* that he invited me for an interview solely so that he could chase me out of the studios. I remember he was chubby, out of condition and red-faced and I thought he was going to have a heart attack.

It was, generally speaking, the jolliest promotional tour I've ever done though I don't think we sold many books.

The best day was spent at Trent Bridge where I recorded a short film for the commercial television station in the English Midlands. The reporter putting the film together had me filmed bowling, batting, wicket-keeping, fielding and umpiring. And then he sat me in the crowd at Trent Bridge during a Test Match and got me to look studious before leaping up to clap enthusiastically. Finally he had me poke my head out of the main score board.

The resultant film, which was a classic in its way, showed me bowling to myself, batting to my own bowling, watching myself and clapping, operating the scoreboard, catching myself and then giving myself out. Cleverly edited, with crowd shots, the whole thing made it look as though I were taking part in a Test Match though we'd filmed the batting, bowling, fielding and umpiring bits in a field where a patch of grass had been carefully turned into a cricket pitch for the occasion. The reporter had even remembered to take a white coat for me to wear while umpiring. There's bound to be a video of it all around somewhere, and I keep meaning to dig it out and put it up on Brand New Tube. It's probably far too controversial to be considered for YouTube.

(It wasn't until I saw *An American in Paris* recently that I remembered that the reporter who had thought up this sequence was probably inspired by a very similar sequence in that film. Oscar Levant, who was a concert pianist, plays a concert pianist and there is a sequence which shows him playing, conducting and generally having a good time with a piano and an orchestra.)

The interviews I really remember, however, didn't take place at all.

I was thrown out of a commentary box at Trent Bridge during a Test Match with a producer snarling at me but the worst was at BBC London. I'd raced across London for an interview at their studios in Marylebone High Street and just managed to get there on time. I was then kept waiting for ages until a very angry little man called Norman de Mosquita came out, red-faced and brandishing my book. 'I just wanted to see you to tell how despicable I thought it was of you to write a spoof of *Wisden*. It's not a subject for humour.' When I asked if he wanted to interview me he said he did not and disappeared just as suddenly as he had arrived. I thought that unprofessional rather than just rude. Oddly, he was apparently a sports reporter who specialised in ice hockey.

Second, I remember an interview which took place at a BBC studio somewhere in the North of England. I was promoting a book called *Bodypower* and I was in the middle of what turned out to be a three week promotion tour. I can't remember where I was but I do vividly remember sitting in a studio opposite a very self-important fellow who had been promoting my forthcoming presence for several hours. (I usually tried to listen to radio stations I was visiting so that I'd have some idea of what was said before I got there.)

'Of course, I shan't mention the title of your book,' he said aggressively, just a minute or so to go before our interview began. Someone in another studio was reading the news.

I stared at him in astonishment. For years it had always been agreed that I (like all touring authors) would give my time without charge while the interviewer/presenter/disk jockey would, in return, give the book/film/new record a decent plug. If it was a long programme the book/film/record would be given several plugs.

'This is the BBC,' he said pompously. 'We don't do advertisements.'

I stared at him with disbelief replacing the astonishment.

'And I don't expect you to mention the title of your book, either,' he added. 'The BBC doesn't do advertisements,' he repeated.

'OK,' I said. 'Then we need to fix a fee. My usual fee for a programme of this type would be £500.'

Now it was his turn to stare at me. 'What fee?' The news ended and another voice started to read the sports news.

'I travelled here on the assumption that you would mention my book,' I told him. 'If you're not going to do that then you will have to pay me. My publisher has train and taxi costs and a hotel bill to pay.'

'Pay you?'

'£500.'

I stood up, put my book and belongings into my bag and made it clear that I was ready to leave.

'I don't have a budget for guests,' he said.

I shrugged and picked up the shoulder bag I always carry with me. Someone was now reading the weather forecast.

'I've promoted you heavily,' he said, plaintively. 'I promoted you yesterday and today.'

'I came because it was assumed that you would mention the title and publisher of my book at least twice: at the beginning of the interview and at the end. But if the BBC has suddenly decided it doesn't do that because it doesn't approve of advertising then I'll have to charge you a fee…which do you prefer?'

The weather forecast ended.

'And now, as promised, my guest today is Vernon Coleman who is here to talk about his new book *Bodypower* which is published by Thames and Hudson…'

Accepting defeat with surprising good grace, he mentioned the title of the book every five minutes. He even gave the price and the name of the publisher.

Being on tour I quickly discovered that I often came across the same authors, actors, musicians and other celebrities who were also on their own promotional tours. We lived in our own little worlds.

My tours never exceeded three weeks in length but I once spent a pleasant afternoon with the actor Simon Ward at some TV studios in Manchester. I was promoting the PAN paperback edition of my book *Stress Control*. He had been touring for six months and had been interviewed on just about every American TV and radio station in existence. He was, I think, promoting his film *Young Winston*. He travelled with a sort of valet, a man who was the ultimate minder and whose job it was to make sure that Simon caught the right trains, had taxis waiting and had hotels booked.

A few minutes after we had both arrived, Simon asked one of the programme researchers if they had a bottle of wine we could share. The researcher disappeared and came back five minutes later to tell us that although they did indeed have a bottle of wine there wasn't a corkscrew in the building. This was a blatant lie, designed to ensure that neither of us got blotto before the programme, but it was a useless lie. Simon's man opened the small suitcase he carried with him and immediately produced a corkscrew. Since neither of us was driving, we then proceeded to get very slightly merry on a couple of bottles of Granada's cheapest wine. By the start of the programme we were the best of friends. By the end of it our first thoughts were to get to our taxis quickly, and to rush to our next interviews as speedily as possible. (Actually, Simon probably had a limousine waiting outside.) I had just three weeks of always rushing to be somewhere else. He had six months of it. On a promotional tour you are never actually anywhere: you are always either just coming from somewhere or you're just going somewhere.

I have no idea how Simon Ward coped with such a long tour, and such an endless number of interviews, but the minder with the small suitcase must have helped make his life infinitely better and definitely jollier.

Walnuts

I don't know how it came about, but we discovered a while ago that the squirrels who share our garden love walnuts. They're very fond of hazelnuts, of course, and peanuts are satisfactory, but they prefer walnuts. They break the nut in half and eat from the two halves of the shell. The size of the nuts means that they are more likely to eat them rather than bury them and forget them.

We buy huge amounts of the nuts from our local greengrocer who buys them throughout the year especially for us.

Naturally, this means that the garden is littered with empty walnut shells.

A tree surgeon arrived to deal with some dead branches and to plant a small new orchard to replace some fruit trees which had matured into kindling and firewood.

'You've got a couple of walnut trees, then?' he said, looking up and around the garden.

'Have we?' I asked, stupidly, looking up and following his gaze.

'Oh yes,' he replied, kicking at half a walnut shell on the ground. 'Here's the evidence.' He looked up and pointed at a sycamore tree. 'I think that's a walnut tree,' he said.

I kicked the walnut shell into the long grass before he could bend down and pick it up.

The walnuts we buy are Californian and all have the exporters logo printed on the shell in red.

My Life as Edward Vernon

When I was still a GP I wrote three novels about a young doctor. My literary agent at the time felt it would confuse the book trade, the reviewers and the reading public (since she was a literary agent she thought of them in that order) if I published the books under my own name, and so I reversed my Christian names and wrote them under the pen name Edward Vernon. Although the books were entirely fiction, they were classified as autobiography because my agent and several editors felt that they would sell better if they were promoted as fact rather than fiction.

(Inevitably journalists and those who write mini biographies on the internet insist that the books were autobiographical because that's what it says in small print on the back of the paperbacks. No amount of arguing can correct this misapprehension so I think I'll let it stay. And Mrs Caldicot was my granny.)

In truth, inventing Edward Vernon was a decision which did little good and merely served to cause confusion among the book trade, the reviewers and the reading public (in that order, of course). And it caused some embarrassment when Pan Books bought the rights to one of my non-fiction books (*Stress Control*) and at the same time bought the rights to my first Edward Vernon book (*Practice Makes Perfect*) without realising that both books were written by the same person. It led to a slightly surreal meeting. (Over the years I have used at least 18 pen names. This is not particularly unusual among authors who do like to reinvent themselves from time to time.)

To begin with it had seemed likely that using a pen name might protect me from the General Medical Council, which in those days had a policy opposed to what it loosely called 'advertising'. Dr Gordon Oslere, the author of the enormously successful *Doctor in the House* series of books had called himself Richard Gordon for the same reason. Sadly, this trick didn't work at all for me. I was threatened by the GMC and it was touch and go for a while whether I would lose my registration. The GMC wasn't much interested in the fact that my medical practice hadn't benefitted at all from my authorship and when I, early on in proceedings, I pointed out to a lawyer from the Medical Defence Union that Dr Richard Gordon didn't seem to have been hassled by the GMC the lawyer, a small, dusty insipid fellow who worked in a windowless office the size of a small, modern wardrobe pointed out that Dr Gordon was very well known and that it was, therefore, quite different. I never quite got my head round that. The office really wasn't much bigger than a wardrobe by the way. There were three pieces of furniture in the room, a desk and two chairs, and when we sat our knees touched. I remember feeling sorry for that poor fellow, a doctor working for the Medical Defence Union, because he had to spend eight hours a day in that little room.

In the end the GMC decided that the 'advertising' rule was antiquated and of little value and so they did away with it, concentrating for a while on doctors who had succeeded in attracting the attention of a Sunday newspaper known as the News of the World. So, my few weeks of worry had a useful end result for other writers and television doctors.

My agent, a rather loud Canadian who had the biggest signature I've ever known, and an ego even bigger, sold the books to Macmillan (for the hardback) and to Pan (for the paperback) and to St Martin's Press in the United States for the United States market. Oh, what heady exciting days those were.

The editor at St Martin's Press was a wonderfully astute American called Tom McCormack who was famous in publishing circles for having turned James Herriot from a low-selling Yorkshire author into an international phenomenon. Inevitably, there was much talk of turning me into the equivalent of James Herriot. I met Mr McCormack at the Connaught Hotel in London (I remember parking my battered Mini Traveller right outside the hotel and leaving it there under the surprisingly benevolent eye of the doorman) and together we went through the MSS as Mr McCormack explained precisely what American audiences enjoyed most. The British publishers then accepted the changes I had made.

St Martin's Press was pleased enough with the newly edited book to commission oil paintings for the jackets and to promote the book across America but then, suddenly, Mr McCormack disappeared. I was told that he'd broken a leg while skiing but I have no idea whether that was true or merely a polite excuse. It is, of course perfectly possible that he didn't think I had produced something to satisfy American audiences after all.

Practice Makes Perfect, the first book in the Edward Vernon series, nearly became a television series because one of my patients was a famous English playwright called David Turner.

David had started his professional life writing scripts for a radio series called The Archers and had become enormously successful with TV dramas. His own plays were performed in the West End and on Broadway. When I was working as a Community Service Volunteer in Liverpool I had reviewed his play 'Semi-Detached' for a local newspaper – the *Liverpool Echo*, I think.

Unbeknownst to me, David heard about the book and wrote a script for a TV film based on the story. He then gave me the script to approve (which I happily did for it was well-written, professionally executed with all the necessary notes to the director included therein, and it was close to the book which was a bonus) and gave it to his agent to sell.

No one was interested.

We were told (and, indeed, later discovered this to be true) that one of the television companies had recently commissioned a TV series about a young doctor in the North of England, and so naturally it was considered that there would not be room for two such series on television.

I don't know what happened to the script (my copy disappeared years ago) but David became an enthusiastic alcoholic. He made very regular trips to his nearest supermarket and always came home pushing a trolley laden with bottles of spirits and wine – much of which he would consume by himself. Not surprisingly he became worse for wear and his behaviour became erratic, unpredictable and rather anti-social at times. I had dined at his home on one occasion and he insisted on presenting me with a copy of Moliere's play *La Malade Imaginaire*. It was a very early copy from a beautifully bound set and my attempts to refuse the gift (and later to return it) were met with anger bordering on rage. I don't know where the book is now but it is probably hiding somewhere with the script which I have mislaid.

In the end, David's playwriting skills were affected by the booze and he slid down the pole he had climbed. He became a scriptwriter for Crossroads, a television soap opera. I was with him one day when he asked me to read a blood splattered page he'd just written. (The blood came from his nose. The alcohol had given him high blood pressure and the high blood pressure gave him nosebleeds and he was so accustomed to these that he just carried on doing whatever he was doing and allowed the nose to drip blood until it stopped.) The page described the events following a plane crashing onto the motel which was the centrepiece of the programme.

'There are a lot of characters I need to get rid of,' he announced. 'This is the quickest way to kill them off.'

I have no idea whether the storyline was used but not long after he went back to writing for The Archers, a popular radio series.

My disappointing experience with the David Turner script was the first of many false hopes, with expectations repeatedly raised and dashed.

There have been at least three scripts of my book *The Man Who Inherited a Golf Course* and two of the first of my Bilbury books. All were written, all resulted in contracts being drawn up and signed and much hope being raised. Bizarrely, the writer and would-be producer of one of the Bilbury scripts insisted on changing the colour of the skin of the young doctor starting work in a Devon village in the 1970s. For the sake of political correctness they made him black. The people with the money thought this to be such an unlikely occurrence that they declined the invitation to finance the movie. None of these scripts resulted in any business.

Like many authors I have been teased many times by film companies who have expressed enthusiasm for my novels, and have talked long and loud about turning one or other of my stories into movies. I used to have a drawer full of contracts offered and signed, options taken and scripts written. This is by no means unusual. There are professional screen writers in existence who have never seen one of their scripts turned into a movie but who have, nevertheless, made a good living out of the industry.

My one success was with *Mrs Caldicot's Cabbage War* which, after several years' gestation, became a splendid movie starring Pauline Collins, John Alderton and Peter Capaldi and a host of other excellent actors and actresses.

It seems a trifle disappointing but it's actually not a bad batting average.

My Career in the Movies

The most interesting film maker, manager, mover and shaker I ever met worked in Wardour Street in London's Soho. Wardour Street was, in the 1970s, the part of London where all film companies collected.

I cannot for the life of me remember why or when I met him but I do remember that sitting in the tiny foyer outside his office were two well-known screen actors and one of the nation's most famous and recognisable disc jockeys. I have no idea why they were there but since I had no idea why I was there either that was fair enough.

A secretary, old enough and wrinkled enough to have played one of the witches in Shakespeare's original production of Macbeth, pecked with two bony fingers and no enthusiasm at an old 'sit up and beg' typewriter.

The mover and shaker and I sat in a huge, oak panelled office and the promises flowed like wine at a wedding. I wish I could remember which book of mine we were discussing but I'm afraid I can't. There were, however, to be a film, a television series and several boxed board games for the Christmas market (I do remember that he was keen on boxed games and the Christmas market). There was no doubt in his mind about the success of these projects and there was much talk of contracts, fees, royalties and, for some reason, exotic locations. By the time I left his office, dizzy with hopes and expectations, I was already worrying about my tax liabilities and wondering if I should find a specialist accountant and form an offshore company. In show-business most promises are like pennies, freely given and rarely treasured. But this man's promises were different in that he believed them even more than I did. Later, much later, I realised why. He had to believe in his promises because they were all he had to sell.

I remember leaving, drunk with expectations, carrying an armful of games and toys which were spinoffs from television shows with which he had been associated. I carried these through London and eventually dumped them in a locker I had in a club in Whitehall where I had been a member for some years. The boxes sat there, untouched, for a decade or more before I found someone to whom I could give them.

The funny thing was that I found out later (entirely by accident) that this fellow had never actually managed to get anything produced. He had looked at many scripts, created much excitement, talked very good talk, made expansive promises and raised considerable amounts of money for his projects. But nothing ever came to fruition.

He made his money by taking 10% here and 15% there from the money he raised. Actors keen for work had queued outside his office and investors (known in the business as 'angels' because 'suckers' is far too rude) had willingly put money into his projects. I can't imagine any of them had hoped to receive much of a return on their investments (or indeed received any of their capital back) but it gave them a chance, a hope, of mingling with show-business people and maybe meeting a warm-hearted chorus girl or two.

I cannot remember this fellow's name (all I can remember with certainty is that his office was at the south end of Wardour Street, on the right hand side heading down towards Shaftesbury Avenue) but the meeting took place in the early 1970s and it wasn't until some years later that I realised that I had inadvertently stumbled into a variation of the plot of Mel Brooks's magnificent film *The Producers*.

So, that's my career in the movies.

Except for *Mrs Caldicot's Cabbage War*, of course.

Anton

When we were living and working in Paris, we met a man called Anton who had what I thought then, and still think, was the strangest job I've ever come across.

Anton was a jolly, comfortably rotund, red-faced man who always seemed to be smiling. He was one of those rare creatures who looked as though he didn't have a care in the world because he really didn't have a care in the world.

He was a professional eater.

I know that sounds difficult to believe but that's what he did for a living: he ate food, good, well-cooked, well-varied French food in a smart restaurant on one of the main boulevards in the heart of Paris. It was one of those restaurants designed to look like a traditional French restaurant and, therefore, catering almost exclusively to tourists. It had red sunshades outside and lots of copper pots and pans decorating the walls. The French, of course, prefer to eat hamburgers in McDonalds.

You've probably heard of people whose job it is to taste teas, or beers or chocolate. Those aren't eaters. They taste and then spit out whatever they are tasting. I read once, in the *New Yorker* magazine about a 25-year-old man who worked in Glasgow, Scotland, and whose job it was to sample all the available malt whiskies and combine them with grain whisky to make consistent and accessible blended whiskies. That wasn't drinking; it was teasing. His body must have been constantly kept in a state of expectation and disappointment.

Anton wasn't paid to taste food and spit it out. He was paid to sit at a nice table in a smart restaurant and eat. And he wasn't a permanent contestant in one of those eating competitions where grimly determined contestants, usually overweight, middle-aged men, compete to see who can eat the most burgers or hot dogs in 30 minutes or an hour.

Anton was hired by the restaurant owner to sit at a small table in the window, select items from the menu and eat them. He would order a three course meal (usually from the a la carte menu but once or twice a day from the fixed menu) and chew his way through everything put in front of him. He would then have a coffee and a small brandy before starting again with another meal. The brandy was the only alcohol he drank. For obvious reasons, he confined himself to bottled water with his meals – the restaurant didn't want him getting tiddly half way through his working day.

I once asked Anton how he'd come to be hired.

He told me that he used to have a job as a cashier in a men's clothing store a block away from the restaurant and that he'd eaten his lunch there two or three times a week, always sitting at a small table for one in the window. A single man, he spent most of his money on rent and food. He had no expensive hobbies or family. He rented a small, one bedroomed apartment on the top floor of a handsome looking 19th century building in Montparnasse.

The restaurant owner, an astute fellow, noticed that when Anton was sitting eating, the people passing by would see him, look, often stop for a moment and then enter the restaurant. One customer, when asked why he had chosen that restaurant, explained that the fat guy in the window really seemed to be enjoying his food.

Anton even looked the part. He had a habit of tucking the white linen napkin, which the restaurant provided, into the top of his shirt. The restaurant owner apparently once said that he thought that this gave him the look of a gourmet. In reality, I thought he would probably be more accurately described as a gourmand. But he was definitely not a glutton. A glutton would have revolted the customers rather than attracted them. Most people take in food with the same general lack of discrimination as they fill their cars with fuel or indeed with which they guzzled on breast milk when they were babies. Gluttons simply don't know when to stop. Anton enjoyed his food, in quantity and quality, and his enjoyment showed.

The owner offered him a job.

All you have to do is sit at your usual seat and eat all day long. All your meals will be free and I'll pay you a salary.'

The salary wasn't much, was in fact slightly less than he'd received as a cashier, but Anton hated his job and loved food and he would save on meals so it took him no time at all to say yes, thank you, when do I start?

At 2.30 pm, as the lunchtime rush came to an end, Anton would get up from his table and go off for a walk and to do a little window shopping. It was, I suppose, the equivalent of a normal person's lunch-break – except, of course, that he didn't eat anything.

I once asked him what he ate on Sundays – his one day off. He told me he always made himself a croquet madame – cheese on toast or opened a can of soup – minestrone being his favourite. If the restaurant had been open on Sundays he would have happily worked seven days a week.

While Anton was away from 'work', enjoying his walk, one of the waiters would put a reserved sign on his table and when he had finished his daily constitutional, Anton would return, sit down, roll up his sleeves (metaphorically only, of course), pick up the menu and order his next meal, eating his way through until 8 pm by which time the restaurant would be full with the evening patrons and he could put on his overcoat and head off home. At least he didn't have to shop for food or worry about cooking himself a meal.

Anton never read while he was eating. The restaurant paid him to eat and to do nothing but eat. Occasionally, he would look out of the window, see potential customers looking in, smile, nod in approval and pop another forkful of food into his mouth. His attitude was that he never read a book or a newspaper while performing his old job so why should he do so in his new job?

The restaurant owner's theory was that the sight of someone eating, and clearly enjoying his food, reminded people that it was time to eat, made them feel hungry and reassured them that the restaurant would look after them well enough. The fact that the space in the window alcove where Anton ate was only big enough for a table for one meant that the restaurant didn't lose a table for two or four.

And then, one day, Anton wasn't at his usual table. Instead, the place was occupied by a morose looking stranger, clearly not hired to eat, who was nibbling at the edges of a plain omelette and reading his newspaper.

Three weeks after his disappearance we met Anton in a café on the Boulevard St Michel. We were on our way to the Luxembourg Gardens and had stopped for an expresso and a cup of tea. Anton was nursing a glass of beer and looked younger, fitter, and much slimmer.

'Where have you been?' I asked. 'We've missed seeing you at

your table.' The restaurant's proximity to our apartment building meant that we passed the window once or twice a day.

'I lost weight,' said Anton. 'The owner didn't think that having a thin man eating his food would bring in the customers.'

'But how could you lose weight?' asked Antoinette. 'You were eating all day long!'

'Nine or ten full meals a day,' he agreed.

'Have you seen your doctor?' I asked.

He said he hadn't.

I told him he should. He really had lost a good deal of weight. I was worried about him. I didn't say anything specific but it seemed possible that he might have developed stomach cancer or something equally unpleasant. He promised that he would.

Two days later we had to go to England to see a close relative who had fallen ill. When the relative had made a good recovery we took the opportunity to travel around a little and see family and friends we hadn't seen for some time.

And so, as a result, we were away from Paris for a month and then, having a good deal to do in order to catch up with the work we'd both missed doing while we had been away, we didn't go anywhere very much for another week or ten days.

With one with one thing and another, it was nearly two months before we next walked past the restaurant where Anton had been employed. To our delight he was back at his usual table, finishing off his post-prandial coffee and brandy. He looked almost as plump as he ever had done. He saw us looking, smiled and waved us to go in to the restaurant.

'Thank you for suggesting that I saw my doctor,' he said. 'He managed to sort things out for me.'

'You seem to be back to your eating weight!' said Antoinette.

'Just a couple of pounds to go,' smiled Anton. 'If I put on another half a stone the boss has promised me a raise!'

'What was wrong with you?' I asked him.

'I had a tapeworm,' he said. 'Thirty foot long,' he added proudly.

Antoinette shuddered.

'Has it gone now?' I asked him.

'Completely,' nodded Anton. 'Passed it whole. The doctor thought it might have been from some beef or pork that was undercooked. We don't do sushi here so it wouldn't have been from raw fish. He gave me some medicine in case the tapeworm had laid any eggs.'

'And you feel OK now?'

'Fit as a fiddle.'

Just then the waiter came to take Anton's order for his next meal. We said goodbye and told him how pleased we were to see him back at work.

'I'd hate to have a tapeworm inside me,' said Antoinette as we continued on our way.

'Did you know there's a tapeworm diet?'

She looked at me in the way that she does when she thinks I'm joking.

'No, really, there is! You can buy tapeworm eggs, or even a small tapeworm in a jar. You swallow the eggs or the tapeworm and then when you've lost all the weight you want to lose you take some medicine to get rid of it.'

'I don't believe you!' laughed Antoinette.

I don't blame her for being sceptical, but it's true.

The Policeman's Shoulder

Visiting patients at home was a regular part of the day when I was a GP. Most of the requests for home visits would come in by telephone while I was doing the morning surgery. Some would be elderly patients with chronic health problems who needed a routine consultation but who found it difficult to get to the surgery for an office consultation. Some would be patients who had just been discharged from hospital, or who were convalescing and needed attention for some reason. Some were chronic invalids. Some were seriously ill but didn't need or want to go into hospital. Visiting them every two weeks meant that when the end came there wouldn't be any need to upset the family with a post-mortem or an inquest.

But most of the visits were for patients who had fallen ill, usually overnight, and who didn't feel well enough to travel to the surgery.

Unless the requests were for an urgent visit (an asthmatic, diabetic, a patient with chest pain, a screaming child with earache and so on) I would do the visits when I had finished the morning surgery, signed letters that had been dictated the previous day, dealt with requests for repeat prescriptions, looked at the correspondence, dictated a few more letters and attempted to deal with whatever staff crises had developed during the morning. (Unlike modern practices which employ dozens of staff members, including managers and human resources specialists, I only had a couple of receptionists to worry about, but there always seemed to be little problems to deal with.)

If I couldn't finish the 'morning' visits before lunch I would finish them afterwards. Other calls for home visits trickled in throughout the day, during lunch, after lunch and on through the evening surgery. At six o'clock at night we would switch the telephones through to the surgery or home of the member of the practice who was on duty for the night. (He would have just finished a full day's work and would work the following day too.)

The evening surgery would usually finish at about seven and unless I was the 'lucky' doctor on call for the night I could go home for the evening and ignore ringing telephones. (Is it any wonder that I now hate telephones, rarely use them and jump six inches into the air if I am anywhere near one when it rings?)

I know that these days, doctors rarely visit patients but I always liked visiting patients in their homes. It was interesting to see how and where people lived, and I found it easier to understand their fears and circumstances if you knew more about them.

Of course, things sometimes went disastrously wrong. And sometimes patients took advantage of the system and demanded a home visit when they could have easily visited the surgery.

Responding to one request for a home visit I knocked on the front door and waited.

And waited.

And waited.

I knocked again.

And waited.

The patient lived in a block of flats so there was no back door.

Eventually, convinced that the patient must have collapsed I went to a neighbour, borrowed her telephone and rang the police. Within minutes there was a squeal of brakes and tyres outside and almost immediately after that a huge policeman appeared, panting, at the top of the flight of stairs up to my patient's flat. He was a patient of mine and although I didn't recognise him he recognised me and we went through the ritual verbal dance which is, I'm sure, well known to many doctors.

'Hello, doctor! That ointment did the trick beautifully.'

'Splendid!' I said, completely unable to remember what ointment I'd given him or why.

'Do you think it'll come back?'

'I wouldn't think so. But if it does, just pop along and I'll take another look.'

'That's great. Thanks doc. When we've finished here do you think you could give me a prescription for some more of my wife's pills?'

I said I would, though this would involve some verbal gymnastics as I endeavoured to find his wife's name, their address and the nature of the pills she was taking. I had found ways to do this without letting on that I couldn't remember any of the information, though the perennial 'Remind me – how do you spell you name?'

looks a trifle thin when the patient replies 'Oh, the usual way, doctor' and you push a little and the patient then spells out 'S-M-I-T-H.'.

The policeman threw himself at the door in what was, I assume, the officially accepted method of shoulder charging a door. The door didn't budge. He was just about to try using one of his size 12 boots to kick down the door when an old lady appeared, with two shopping bags.

'What are you doing?' the missing patient demanded, rather irately.

I explained that we thought she must have collapsed in her flat.

'I've been out to do a bit of shopping,' she told us, rather indignantly.

She'd had to walk past my surgery on the way to the shops.

I waited, fuming, while she found her keys. I had a long list of visits to do.

'When you've dealt with the old lady, would you mind taking a look at my shoulder, doctor? I hurt it when I tried to knock that door down.'

There was nothing wrong with the old lady except that she wanted a repeat prescription for some arthritis medicine.

The policeman I had to send to hospital for an X-ray. It turned out later that he'd cracked his collar bone.

On Getting Old

I don't know if this applies to everyone, or is something to which I can claim an element of exclusivity, but as I have grown older I have become increasingly aware that there may (indeed probably are) things going on about which I have no knowledge but which may, or will, affect my life in some quite dramatic fashion.

Is there a cancer starting to grow within my doubtless already oversized prostate gland? Is my pancreas wearing out? Is my liver struggling to stand on its own two feet (metaphorically speaking)? Are my coronary arteries furring up in the way that all old pipes are prone to fur up? Is a journalist researching for an attack on me? Is a lawyer preparing a writ?

I am, inevitably perhaps, aware that time is running out and I am, therefore, a little more careful in how I look after the hours and the days. Look after the hours and the days, and the months will look after themselves. I have become increasingly intolerant of rude and selfish people who, through a lack of care or natural human respect, wilfully waste my time. I have always been intolerant of the variety of rudeness which manifests itself in that way but I suspect that feeling has become more pronounced. The less of anything we have the more valuable it becomes to us and this is as true of time as of anything else. Maybe this explains why those of more advanced years have a reputation for impatience, which often, to the outsider manifests itself as apparent grouchiness. (I admit that my vices have always included impatience, impulsiveness and excess touchiness.)

We all start life with a terminal illness (death being an inevitability since the human body has built in obsolescence) and the number of things I want to do seem to increase in inverse proportion to the amount of time left in which to do them.

When we are young we squander time because we think that we have all the time in the world to do everything we want to do. Consequently we fritter away the most valuable gift we are given.

To me every hour is now exceptionally valuable because I am aware there aren't all that many of them left. I am not prepared willingly to waste any of my precious hours on bureaucrats, administrators, lawyers, tax inspectors or weeds.

All this sounds rather negative but it isn't (or need not be) because an increased awareness of the ticking of the clock (or, as filmmakers would have it, fluttering pages on the calendar) can give an impetus to get on with things, rather than to prevaricate, and give inspiration to the inclination to think big rather than to be satisfied with small ambitions.

Oh, and I find that I am more cautious when going up and down steps than I used to be.

Parties

I haven't been to a party since I was six-years-old. Parties are clearly dangerous since all the others who attended that party with me are now dead.

Time

It's funny how our attitude to time has changed over the years. These days, people pay huge amounts of money to upgrade their computers and mobile telephones, largely because the replacement they are buying does things a fraction of a second faster. I can't see how this can possibly make a notable difference to anyone who isn't a commodities trader trying to beat the system.

It was, I think, Henry David Thoreau who first pointed out the importance of knowing how long you'd had to work (in other words how much of your life you'd had to sacrifice) in order to buy a new suit of clothes. Or maybe it was William Cobbett. It was his sort of thought. It may, indeed, have been me. I certainly remember, decades ago, pointing out (possibly in my book *Toxic Stress* and equally possibly in a book called *Mind over Body*) how important it is to know how much of your life you'd had to sacrifice (particularly if you hate your job) to buy a new hat (when you already owned a perfectly serviceable hat) or a new car (when there was nothing much wrong with the old one).

Most people ignore this advice, of course, which is their prerogative, and work long hours to buy a better lawnmower or mousetrap, or to be able to afford a flashy holiday they wouldn't need if they didn't work themselves to a standstill. I wonder how many people kill themselves struggling to impress the neighbours they never have time to speak to, except to mention their holiday plans.

People used to be far more sanguine about time.

In our hallway at home there stands an early 17th century long case clock (the sort usually known as a grandfather clock). It is our only heirloom and it had been in my father's family for generations. The clock is unusual in that it only has one hand.

It wasn't until 1650 that it became usual to put two hands on a clock. Before the middle of the 17th century, clock mechanisms weren't accurate enough to measure time by the minute and, besides, most people didn't fuss over minutes and seconds in the way that we do now.

You might think that a one handed clock must be quite valuable. It is certainly rare.

Unfortunately, rare and valuable don't always go together and I suspect that our clock isn't worth very much at all.

The ageing great aunt who bequeathed the clock to the aunt who left it to my father was concerned that the elegantly inscribed clock-face looked rather grimy.

So she gave it a good scrub.

With a wire wool pad.

The wire removed the patina of centuries and left the face scratched beyond repair.

Wire wool might be an excellent way to improve the appearance of a tired saucepan or stove but it's not quite the approved restoration tool for a 350-year-old clock.

Still, the mortally damaged clock is a constant reminder that although we need to cherish every moment of our lives we don't always need to measure everything we do by the minute.

Sometimes 'a bit before seven' or 'something after six' will do just as well, and is all we need.

A Night at the Cavern

When I was working as a Community Service Volunteer in Liverpool in 1964-5 (a year I took off between leaving school and starting medical school) I earned some money by reviewing plays for the local paper and by writing articles for a variety of magazines and newspapers.

Generally, I used to hammer the articles out on very cheap thin copy paper (the paper was usually pink I seem to remember, probably because I'd spotted a bargain and had bought a few reams of the stuff) using my sit up and beg finger mangling typewriter. The machine used to bite and chew my fingers so much that I reckon that every thousand words cost me at least a thimbleful of blood.

As I became a little more successful I occasionally plucked up the courage to telephone a news editor or a features editor on one of the national newspapers to try to sell them a story in advance. Since mobile telephones hadn't been invented, didn't have personal access to a telephone and I didn't want to be constantly feeding coins into a phone box (phone cards hadn't been invented then either) I simply telephoned and reversed the charges.

I don't know how I found out that you could do this but you could. All the national newspaper phone operators would accept reverse charge calls and even though they sometimes asked who was calling they still accepted the call. The papers had huge staffs in the 1960s with hundreds of reporters on staff. There was no way a phone operator could know the names of all the staff members. Back then there were many full-time staff journalists who considered themselves to be doing well if they managed to get a story in the paper once every six months. And the papers were always eager to hear from members of the public who had a story to sell them.

On the 31st March 1965 I discovered that a television special was being broadcast live from the Cavern club in Liverpool. The line-up was pretty spectacular and included Gerry and the Pacemakers, Manfred Mann, Sandie Shaw, Petula Clark and Gene Vincent. Not having the foggiest idea how to get hold of a ticket I rang the *Daily*

Mirror news desk and asked if they wanted me to cover the event for them.

And so, a little later, I turned up at the Cavern, told them I was representing the *Daily Mirror* and was allowed in without a ticket, a press pass or anything except a pencil stub and a cheap notebook to guarantee my intentions.

The programme was a live co-production with the BBC and a French TV station and I can still remember parts of it. Gene Vincent sang a duet with a jazz singer called Nancy Holloway who was in Paris. He was still suffering from the injuries sustained in the accident that had killed 21-year-old Eddie Cochran and he sang leaning up against the wall. Sandie Shaw came down the steps into the cavern and took off her shoes just before she reached the bottom. Someone walking behind her, and just out of shot, picked them up. When Petula Clark rehearsed her huge international hit Downtown, the small crowd became restless and the director, whose name I cannot remember, threatened to clear the club if we didn't all behave. He couldn't have done that, of course, since he needed an audience for the show. We all knew that but we were polite and pretended he could.

After the show I made my way up to the dressing rooms and found myself talking to Manfred Mann, Paul Jones and Sandie Shaw. I missed the scoop of the night when Manfred Mann told me that he wanted to give up making singles because of the stress of waiting to see if the band's last record was a hit or not.

I wrote a short piece about the event for the *Daily Mirror* and I think they printed about two inches of it. I wrote a couple of pieces about it for other papers and magazines. There were, I think, just two of us there reporting on the event. The other representative of the press was the editor of a small local Liverpool paper who seemed slightly bemused by the whole thing. He and I both wore jackets and ties and we were not alone in this.

Those were simpler days.

The First Television

When I was small we had the first television in our street. We weren't well off but my Dad made the set, using an article in a magazine for directions and buying all the bits from a local shop. Can you imagine finding a shop today where you could buy all the bits to make a television set?

I remember being woken up, taken into the kitchen and shown the TV set sitting on our kitchen table. It had no cabinet and a small screen and all the valves and so on were visible. My Dad and my Mum were, rightly, very proud. I was no more than four-years-old and it is one of my first memories. We were living in a prefab in Bloxwich, Walsall at the time. Prefabs, bungalows made out of sheets of something which looked like asbestos, and probably was, were put up after the Second World War on just about any piece of available land. They took about five minutes to erect (with a three minute tea break included) and couldn't have cost more than a tenner to make. I think my parents probably got one because my Dad had been in the Navy throughout the War and had been invalided out with a stomach ulcer. He'd been on three ships which had all been torpedoed and all been sunk in the Atlantic. That, together with Navy food, would have probably given anyone an ulcer.

Shortly after the building of their first TV set, my parents bought their first house. It was a detached three bedroom house, very smart, in a posh part of Walsall and they paid around £2,500 for it. It had a large garden which came complete with two air raid shelters and two greenhouses. I think the former owner, a builder, had had a very symmetrical sort of mind. Who else would build a pair of matching air raid shelters?

The television set came with us and we had to have an H shaped aerial fixed on the roof so that we could pick up programmes.

Very few homes had aerials in the early 1950s and the occupants of those houses which did possess an aerial were considered very special. It quickly became fairly common for people without TV sets to have aerials put onto the roofs. It was cheaper to have an aerial put on the roof than to buy a TV set and the social cachet was the same.

A year or two later my Dad, who had become keen on 'doing it himself', put central heating into the house. This was quite a boon because before the central heating was installed he had to pour kettles full of water onto the bathroom pipes in order to melt the ice that formed. My bedroom windows were all covered with the wonderful patterns of ice which showed that Jack Frost had visited during the night.

I remember my Dad digging up the floorboards and putting in all the pipes and radiators. The boiler had to be fed with something called anthracite which was delivered by men who periodically trudged up and down our driveway carrying bags of the stuff. The anthracite was stored in one of the old air raid shelters in the garden. This could only be reached by climbing up and down a tricky flight of stairs. So the delivery men took the anthracite down the steps and my Dad then had to carry the stuff back up to the house as and when it was needed. Once it had been carried back up to the house, it was poured into the boiler which had a ravenous appetite and was never content.

I mention the central heating because once it was working ours was the first house in the street to have a roof without snow or frost on it on the coldest days of winter. (In those days, before climate change had been popularised, it used to be considered normal for the weather to be cold in the winter and warm in the summer.) All the other houses, none of which had central heating, had roofs covered in snow. The red tiles on our house were completely free of snow. This marked us out as rather special because it made it clear that we were blessed with central heating.

Gradually the other houses had central heating installed and after a few years all the neighbouring houses had snow covered roofs on icy winter days.

And then someone discovered lagging.

Once again my Dad was the first to do it himself. He covered the floor of the loft with rolls of asbestos to keep the warmth from our boiler confined to the house. The asbestos lagging meant that we now had snow on our roof again in the winter. I remember that the asbestos made us all cough a good deal while it was being carried and rolled into position but it did the same thing to everyone so, sensibly, we thought nothing of it. Both my parents were in their late eighties when they succumbed to diseases which had nothing to do with the asbestos.

And the whole social saga went through another cycle.

My Networking Skills

I have always been utterly useless at networking, making useful contacts, nurturing them and benefitting from them.

Once or twice, early in my career, before it became known that I am not a sociable sort of person, publishers organised launch parties for me. The idea was that I would wander around the room speaking to journalists and other important people about myself and the book I was supposed to be promoting. There would usually be acidic white wine to drink and bits of cheese and pineapple on cocktail sticks to eat. The journalists mostly drank the wine and left the bits of cheese and pineapple on cocktail sticks. In those days journalists would drink anything described as wine.

I always spent these events in a corner, speaking to no one. Occasionally, my editor or a salesman or marketing person would come and talk to me and bring me a glass of wine or a pair of cubes of cheese and pineapple on a small skewer. I would pour the wine into a pot plant (there was always a pot plant in the corner in those days) and stuff the cheese and pineapple into my pocket to be discarded later.

Gold medal quality shyness has always meant I've always just disappeared behind the furniture when I should have been pressing flesh and exchanging phone numbers. On at least two of these occasions, the only person I spoke to all evening was my editor. I don't think that's what they mean by 'networking'.

When I was young I used to be able to find the courage to ring a newspaper or magazine office, or to send in an article 'on spec', but as the years went by my courage disappeared and after the age of 25 just about every serious job I ever had with a newspaper or television station came because they contacted me rather than the other way around.

My greatest non-networking achievement took place inside Buckingham Palace. I'd been invited to a shindig there because I had been the first Community Service Volunteer in the country. At least, Alec Dickson, the fellow who founded CSV, told me that I had been the very first and he probably knew.

The place was awash with Important People and a smattering of former volunteers. My Mum was proud because I had my picture taken on the famous front door steps and I was chuffed to bits because I was sent a car park sticker entitling me to park in the courtyard of Buckingham Palace.

Once inside the place I was attacked by an acute attack of shyness. I found what seemed like a small chapel, probably the room where they do investitures, squeezed onto a pew and stayed there. Moments later, the Prime Minister, Margaret Thatcher came and stood about two or three feet away from me. We exchanged smiles but no words. Curiously, she looked as lost as I felt. I could have lobbied her for a Royal Commission or something useful but I didn't say a word. And nor did she. That was my networking strike one for the evening. Anyone with an ounce of networking skill would have gouged a knighthood out of a lonely looking Margaret Thatcher.

Strike two came a few moments later when I was invited to stand in a short line to meet HM Queen Elizabeth II. I think the proper term is 'being presented at court' and it's deemed better than an invitation to a garden party because it is more intimate and it happens indoors where it doesn't rain and there are fewer wasps.

True to form, I snuck away and hid in the loo and then quietly retrieved my car and drove home.

Not bad going.

I managed to avoid speaking to the Prime Minister and the Queen of England in the space of a couple of hours.

How's that for a networking failure?

Keith Miller

Modern professional sports persons are constantly complaining about the stress they are under. It is becoming increasingly common for players to walk away for a while, in order to take time off to recover from the intolerable pressure they say they are under. Many earn unbelievably huge sums of money and are garlanded with honours galore. But still they complain.

Whenever I hear a sports person complaining of the pressure I am reminded of Keith Miller, one of the greatest of all Australian cricketers.

Miller, who had served with distinction as a fighter pilot during World War II, was asked by a young reporter called Michael Parkinson about the pressure of playing in a Test Match.

Miller looked straight at Parkinson and replied: 'I'll tell you what pressure is. Pressure is having a Messerschmitt up your arse. Playing cricket is not.'

The Gallows

I had forgotten all about it until I started to write this book but shortly after I arrived in Birmingham to start my medical studies I was contacted by Community Service Volunteers (the organisation through which I had just finished the best part of a year working as a volunteer in Liverpool) and asked if I would help set up some sort of night club in Birmingham. I expect most first year medical students get similar phone calls.

There was, it seemed, virtually nowhere for the young people of Britain's second city to go if they didn't have much money and weren't students somewhere. (Birmingham was officially described as Britain's second city at the time.)

Somehow, I was offered the use of a large unoccupied building in the centre of the city. I had no staff and no furniture – nothing apart from a large, empty building which had a small coffee bar attached to it. The only rule was that I wasn't allowed to serve alcohol in the building. I think the people who owned the building disapproved of alcohol.

Within a surprisingly short time I had managed to recruit a number of students to help out, found a disc jockey prepared to play records for a small fee and recruited a couple of bands prepared to play live music for similarly small fees. Finding the money for these small fees and buying some records and equipment on which to play them was something of a problem because the person who owned the lease was taking all the profit from the coffee bar and I had decided that in order to make the whole thing accessible there would be no entrance fee.

Discounting the financial problem (which loomed so large that I ignored it for the time being) the first requirement was to arrange some publicity so that we had some customers. From my articles and columns I had just enough money to pay for some leaflets to be printed. My volunteers agreed to wander around Birmingham handing these out to likely 'customers' and (illegally) sticking them wherever they could stick them without being arrested.

The next problem was to find some sort of seating so that people not wanting to dance could sit down. Buying or renting chairs was impossibly expensive but I somehow managed to get hold of a pile of old beds (some bedsteads and rather more mattresses than mattresses). I got these free because the person who owned them wanted to get rid of them. These we distributed around the hall, innocently thinking that they would make an excellent substitute for chairs.

The second problem was that the building's lighting consisted entirely of fluorescent tubes that produced a stark and definitely unsuitable light. I managed to get round this by turning these off and leaving on a few emergency lights – the sort that have EXIT written on them. I also borrowed an epidiascope from the medical school. The word 'borrowing' is perhaps something of an exaggeration because I didn't know who to ask if I could borrow it (and rather suspected that permission would not be forthcoming) so I just, sort of, took it. It wasn't stealing because I intended to take it back every night after it had been used. I didn't think any member of the University staff was likely to attend and spot the epidiascope being used. I also managed to 'borrow' a projector suitable for films. One of the volunteers borrowed some sort of vehicle in which we could transport these items between the medical school and the hall, which was now known as 'The Gallows' and partly decorated with paintings of skeletons and body parts.

We then struck a lucky vein.

First, the *Evening Mail* (a big evening paper in Birmingham) ran a story about the new disco being opened in the city. The paper mentioned that beds were being placed around and on the dance floor.

Second, a number of city councillors, spotting an opportunity for some self-serving publicity, were shocked that beds should be placed within a building. They decided that I was organising something definitely disreputable and announced that I or The Gallows, and possibly both, should be banned, arrested, excommunicated or put into the stocks.

At this point, I admit that things did get rather out of hand.

Perhaps foolishly, I then did a number of interviews, describing our plans. One of the interviews was for an evening show on the BBC Light Programme. (This was long before the BBC gave its stations numbers.) On the programme I inadvertently mentioned that we would be using an epidiascope and a film projector to provide added entertainment. I think I might have added that slides of human tissue, when projected onto the ceiling, produced wonderfully colourful patterns. And that we intended to use the film projector to project old black and white comedies onto the ceiling at the same time. I probably didn't bother to mention that the mixture was definitely psychedelic.

The next morning I received a message commanding me to visit the Dean of the Medical School who wished to speak to me.

When I arrived I was rather dismayed to see that he had my file on his desk. Moreover it was about three inches thick. I still don't know what was in it. I hadn't been aware I had aroused so much attention. I'd only been at the medical school for a matter of months.

Unfortunately, the Dean turned out to be a listener to the Light Programme and had heard my interview on the BBC. He wanted to know where I had obtained the epidiascope I was using in my disco. He pointed out that it seemed unlikely that I happened to have such an expensive piece of equipment in my possession.

I had little choice but to confess.

Another few pages were added to my file but, strangely, I was not told that I could not continue 'borrowing' the epidiascope. I took the double negative to be a positive.

(The Dean had a rather loud bark but an understanding nature. Another student of my acquaintance once 'borrowed' a double decker bus when he found that the last bus home had gone. The police didn't have any difficulty in finding the bus because he had parked it in the road outside. The police wanted to prosecute but the Dean persuaded them to leave matters to him. He was similarly broad minded about the 'borrowed' grit bin, left parked so that those with motor cars would have access to grit for a rather steep local road and pavement. These days these antics would have led to expulsions. My year at medical school had around 100 students in it. I doubt if more than 10 would have survived the five year course if today's disciplinary procedures had been followed.)

After that things went surprisingly smoothly. I don't know whether the dean intervened with them or the council changed its mind but no one turned up to arrest us when we opened.

I realised that the only way I could make any money to pay for the DJ and the band and for bus fares home for the students helping out was to charge a fee for people to use the cloakroom. So, two students were put in charge and we charged a few shillings for parking coats. We had hundreds of customers and the take from the cloakroom was enough to cover all our costs. In the summer the take fell considerably so I had to learn to live on the fat from the winter.

At the time I was also reviewing plays for the *Birmingham Post* and, as I've mentioned earlier in this book, this entitled me to use the *Birmingham Post's* taxi contract free of charge. On nights when I was reviewing a play I used the taxi service to take home the volunteers from the discotheque. This worked well until the Assistant Editor, Leslie Duckworth, wanted to know why the taxi I'd used to take me home after an evening's reviewing had driven round most of the Birmingham area and had stopped at nine separate destinations. Not being able to think of a fictitious explanation I confessed. He told me not to do it again.

The only other serious problem was that a dozen or so youths who attended the disco took to living in the building because they had nowhere else to sleep. Most of them carried knives and were rather boisterous. One of the chores at the end of an evening was cleaning blood off the floor.

Since I was supposed to be running the place one or two of the youths targeted me, testing my authority by showing me their knives.

Fortunately, not only had I just spent the best part of a year working with gangs in what was then considered to be the toughest part of Liverpool, but I had taken to going everywhere with a Victorian swordstick I had purchased from an antique shop in the city centre. The stick contained a very vicious looking blade that was about two and a half feet long. When I was approached by youths showing me their knives, and expecting me to run away, I pulled the sword out of its ebony sheath.

Instant respect.

It was a moment unknowingly reprised years later by Paul Hogan in the film Crocodile Dundee rather more than 20 years later.

But I have to say that my blade was considerably bigger than Mr Hogan's.

I had absolutely no trouble with the knife carriers after that.

Indeed, on the odd occasions when outside, gangs tried to muscle in and cause trouble I found that my 'gang' was enthusiastic in their defence of me and The Gallows. Having the biggest blade in town seemed to be a simple but solid sign of leadership.

I've still got the swordstick though these days I never take it out of the house since it is classified as an offensive weapon. I gather that carrying it is illegal and could lead to a spell sewing mailbags, making number plates or taking part in whichever activities are deemed suitable for those in custody these days.

Extra 1: The Best Diaries

Autobiographies and diaries only work if the writer is unselfconscious and brutally honest. And has a sense of humour. And isn't pompous.

The autobiographies and diaries which sell best are, invariably, the ones written by celebrities. But they are only rarely truly entertaining. The best diaries I've discovered are the ones written by the authors listed below:

James Agate
James Fothergill
James Lee-Milne
Simon Gray
Michael Wharton
P.G. Wodehouse

Extra 2: Books to Read

There is no progress in art. There is only change. There is some progress in science (computers get smaller and faster) but today's writers don't write better books or plays than Dickens, Shakespeare, Trollope or Ambler

With a mixture of ambition, hope and faith I have made a list of authors I want to start to re-read. The obvious ones include Dickens, Wells, Hemingway, Maugham, Waugh, Bennett, Defoe and Goldsmith. I am also re-reading the best thriller writers. I have already worked my way through Eric Ambler and some Graham Greene. I have everything ever written by John Buchan, John Le Carre, Adam Hall, Brian Freemantle, Ross Thomas (and the books he wrote as Oliver Bleeck), Lawrence Block (under all his pen names), Donald E. Westlake (under his enormous variety of pennames), Clive Egleton, Robert Campbell, Robert B. Parker, Charles McCarry and Robert Littell. The novels of Louis L'Amour are massively under-rated. I finished re reading all the books by P.G.Wodehouse a few months ago but with over 90 titles to read I can start them again shortly. And then there are the wonderful books by Jerome K. Jerome, H.E.Bates, Nancy Mitford and Beverley Nichols and the Hornblower books by C.S.Forester. I've got everything written by Simenon, Thurber, Benchley, Jerome K Jerome, Leacock, and Deighton and T.H.White. It used to be difficult to find books by favourite authors. Fifty years ago I discovered Ross Macdonald, widely regarded as the most accomplished American thriller writer of them all, superior even to Raymond Chandler and Dashiel Hammett, but it was nigh on impossible to find copies of his books. I completely forgot about him for half a century and rediscovered him recently. It is now extremely easy to buy them on the internet. I ought to mention, I suppose, that I strongly suspect that some of these authors are now regarded as unacceptable. A good many great authors have been branded unsuitable because their style and approach was better fitted to an earlier time. Buchan, Dickens and Shakespcare are regarded as unacceptable to many because they are considered politically incorrect. But books are important because they relate to a particular time and reflect the mores and culture of that time. So I shall read whatever I want to read, thank you very much. And if God is generous and I get through all those, there are many thousands of other good books in my library. I know there are people who never read a book twice – considering it a waste of their time to do so. But there is nothing wrong with comfort reading. If you are reading to escape from the real world then the only thing that matters is that the book provides an opportunity to do just that. It must capture the imagination. Books give relief from the torment of too much anxiety. Finding new authors which do this takes time and trial and effort. I find that books provide the greatest relief when they are part of a series with a character with whom it is easy to develop a rapport – like Quiller, Charlie Muffin, Smiley, Travis McGee, Spenser and so on and on. I confess that I much enjoyed writing my own series of books. There are 15 books in the Bilbury series and I have written four about Mrs Caldicot. The characters in both series are firm friends and, laugh if you will, but I do think of them as real people. If you think those are shameless plugs then you are probably right.

This list only includes fiction but, of course, many non-fiction books are well worth re-reading.

Extra 3: Biography of the Author

Vernon Coleman was an angry young man for as long as it was decently possible. He then turned into an angry middle-aged man. And now, with no effort whatsoever, he has matured into being an angry old man. He is, he confesses, just as angry as he ever was. Indeed, he may be even angrier because, he says, the more he learns about life the more things he finds to be angry about.

Cruelty, prejudice and injustice are the three things most likely to arouse his well-developed sense of ire but he admits that, at a pinch, inefficiency, incompetence and greed will do almost as well.

The author has an innate dislike of taking orders, a pathological contempt for pomposity, hypocrisy and the sort of unthinking political correctness which attracts support from *Guardian* reading pseudo-intellectuals. He also has a passionate loathing for those in authority who do not understand that unless their authority is tempered with compassion and a sense of responsibility the end result must always be an extremely unpleasant brand of totalitarianism.

Vernon Coleman qualified as a doctor in 1970 and has worked both in hospitals and as a principal in general practice. He has organised many campaigns concerning iatrogenesis, drug addiction and the abuse of animals, and has given evidence to committees at the House of Commons and the House of Lords. Dr Coleman's campaigns have often proved successful. For example, after a 15 year campaign (which started in 1973) he eventually persuaded the British Government to introduce stricter controls governing the prescribing of benzodiazepine tranquillisers. 'Dr Vernon Coleman's articles, to which I refer with approval, raised concern about these important matters,' said the Parliamentary Secretary for Health in the House of Commons in 1988.

Coleman has worked as a columnist for numerous national newspapers including *The Sun*, *The Daily Star*, *The Sunday Express*, *The Sunday Correspondent* and *The People*. He once wrote three columns at the same time for national papers (he wrote them under three different names, Dr Duncan Scott in *The Sunday People*, Dr James in *The Sun* and Dr Vernon Coleman in the *Daily Star*). At the same time he was also writing weekly columns for the *Evening Times* in Glasgow and for the *Sunday Scot*. His syndicated columns have appeared in over 50 regional newspapers. His columns and articles have appeared in newspapers and magazines around the world, and he has contributed articles and stories to hundreds of other publications including *The Sunday Times*, *Observer*, *Guardian*, *Daily Telegraph*, *Sunday Telegraph*, *Daily Express*, *Daily Mail*, *Mail on Sunday*, *Daily Mirror*, *Sunday Mirror*, *Punch*, *Woman*, *Woman's Own*, *The Lady*, *Spectato*r and *British Medical Journal*. He was the founding editor of the *British Clinical Journal*.

For many years he wrote a monthly newsletter. He has lectured doctors and nurses on a variety of medical matters. Tens of millions have consulted his telephone advice lines, watched his videos and visited his websites.

He has presented numerous programmes on television and radio and was the original breakfast television doctor. He was television's first agony uncle (on BBC1's The Afternoon Show) and presented three TV series based on his bestselling book *Bodypower*. In the now long-gone days when producers and editors were less wary of annoying the establishment, he was a regular broadcaster on many radio and television programmes.

In recent years he has worried many parts of the establishment, and today he is widely banned from television and radio and his books are no longer reviewed in newspapers where editors hope to be remembered in the honours lists.

In the 1980s, he wrote the algorithms for the first computerised health programmes — which sold around the world (or, at least, in 26 countries) to those far-sighted individuals who had bought the world's first home computers.

His books have been published in the UK by Arrow, Pan, Penguin, Corgi, Mandarin, Star, Piatkus, RKP, Thames and Hudson, Sidgwick and Jackson, Macmillan and many other leading publishing houses and translated into 25 languages. English language versions sell in the USA, Australia, Canada and South Africa as well as the UK. Several of his books have appeared on both the *Sunday Times* and *Bookseller* bestseller lists. His books have sold over two million copies in the UK, been translated into 25 languages and now sell in over 50 countries. His bestselling non-fiction book *Bodypower* was voted one of the 100 most popular books of the 1980s/90s and was turned into two television series in the UK. His novel *Mrs Caldicot's Cabbage War* has been filmed and is, like many of his other novels, available in an audio version.

Coleman has, in addition, written numerous articles (and many books) under a vast variety of pennames (some of which he has now forgotten). When he feels tired (which happens with increasing frequency) his wife reminds him of all this and he sometimes feels better for a little while. Vernon Coleman's work has also been included in many anthologies including the Penguin Book of 21st Century Protest. He has contributed to various encyclopaedias.

Vernon Coleman has worked for the Open University in the UK and was an honorary Professor of Holistic Medical Sciences at the Open International University based in Sri Lanka. He has received lots of rather jolly awards from people he likes and respects. He is, for example, a Knight Commander of The Ecumenical Royal Medical Humanitarian Order of Saint John of Jerusalem, a Knight Commander of the Knights of Malta and a member of the Ancient Royal Order of Physicians dedicated to His Majesty King Buddhadasa. In 2000, he was awarded the Yellow Emperor's Certificate of Excellence as Physician of the Millennium by the Medical Alternativa Institute.

He has never had a proper job (in the sense of working for someone else in regular, paid employment, with a cheque or pay packet at the end of the week or month) but he has had freelance and temporary employment in many forms. He has, for example, had employment as: postman, fish delivery van driver, production line worker, chemical laboratory assistant, author, publisher, draughtsman, meals on wheels driver, feature writer, drama critic, magician's assistant, book reviewer, columnist, surgeon, police surgeon, industrial medical officer, social worker, night club operator, property developer, magazine editor, general practitioner, private doctor, television presenter, radio presenter, agony aunt, university lecturer, casualty doctor and care home assistant.

Today, he likes books, films and writing. He writes, reads and collects books and has a larger library than most towns. He has never been much of an athlete, though he once won a certificate for swimming a width of the public baths in Walsall and once swam a mile for charity. He finished after everyone else had gone home and had switched off the lights.

Coleman likes pens and notebooks and used to enjoy watching cricket until the authorities sold out and allowed people to paint slogans on the grass. His interests and hobbies include animals, books, photography, drawing, chess, backgammon, cinema, philately, billiards, sitting in cafés and on benches and collecting Napoleana and old books that were written and published before dust-wrappers were invented. He likes log fires and bonfires, motor racing and music by Beethoven, Mozart and Mahler and dislikes politicians, bureaucrats and cauliflower cheese.

Vernon Coleman has co-written five books with his wife, Donna Antoinette Coleman who is a talented oil painter whose work has been exhibited. She is the author of My Quirky Cotswold Garden.

Vernon and Antoinette Coleman have been married for more than 20 years and they live in the delightful if isolated village of Bilbury in Devon where he and his wife have designed for themselves a unique world to sustain and nourish them in these dark and difficult times. He enjoys malt whisky, toasted muffins and old films.

Vernon is devoted to Donna Antoinette who is the kindest, sweetest, most sensitive woman a man could hope to meet. He can ride a bicycle and swim, though not at the same time.

Extra 4: References (Included to counter some of the lies on the internet)

Reference Articles referring to Vernon Coleman
Ref 1
'Volunteer for Kirkby' – The Guardian, 14.5.1965
(Article re VC's work in Kirkby, Liverpool as a Community Service Volunteer in 1964-5)
Ref 2
'Bumbledom forced me to leave the NHS' – Pulse, 28.11.1981
(Vernon Coleman resigns as a GP after refusing to disclose confidential information on sick note forms)
Ref 3
'I'm Addicted To The Star' – The Star, 10.3.1988
Ref 4
'Medicine Becomes Computerised: Plug In Your Doctor.' – The Times, 29.3.1983
Ref 5
'Computer aided decision making in medicine' – British Medical Journal, 8.9.1984 and 27.10.1984
Ref 6
'Conscientious Objectors' – Financial Times magazine, 9.8.2003

Major interviews with Vernon Coleman include:
'Doctor with the Common Touch.' – Birmingham Post, 9.10.1984
'Sacred Cows Beware: Vernon Coleman publishing again.' – The Scotsman, 6.12.1984
'Our Doctor Coleman Is Mustard' – The Sun, 29.6.1988
'Reading the mind between the lines.' – BMA News Review, November 1991
Doctors' Firsts – BMA News Review, 21.2.1996
'The big league of self publishing.' – Daily Telegraph, 17.8.1996
'Doctoring the books' – Independent, 16.3.1999
'Sick Practices' – Ode Magazine, July/August 2003

'You have been warned, Mr Blair.' – Spectator, 6.3.2004 and 20.3.2004
'Food for thought with a real live Maverick.' – Western Daily Press, 5.9.2006
'The doctor will see you now' – Independent, 14.5.2008

There is a more comprehensive list of reference articles on www.vernoncoleman.com

Extra 5: A Note about the Typeface

It is now popular for pretentious authors to include at the back of the books they write a historical note about the typeface which has been chosen for their creation. Well, the typeface used in this book is small, but hopefully not too small, and black. The paper is white stuff, just thick enough so that the reader can't see through it but not so thick that the book is heavy to lift and carry around. And that's about it. Oh, and a few misprints and other errors have been fitted in so that keen eyed and eager proof-reading types can find extra satisfaction within the text. Any such errors which are found were put there deliberately for this purpose. Thank you for caring.

Final Note from the Author:

If you found this book informative I would be very grateful if you would put a suitable review online. It helps more than you can imagine. If you disliked the book, or disapproved of it in any way, please forget you read it.
Vernon Coleman